Great Book by an Exemplary Entrepreneur: Five Stars
Review of <u>The Business of Home Building</u>, by José M. Berlanga

Entrepreneurs are the engine of our vibrant, robust U.S. economy. Without them, we just wouldn't have all the wonderful technology and fantastic goods and services that make our lives so much easier and better. Entrepreneurs are scarce, but they are special people, and we need more of them. An entrepreneur finds opportunities where others don't see them, and goes on to create a successful product or service that meets previously unmet needs. José Berlanga is one of the best examples of an entrepreneur I've ever met. He was in my economics class at the University of Saint Thomas several decades ago, and I vividly remember him and his drive to create a product or service that would make people's lives better. He has done just that by becoming a successful homebuilder in a very competitive market. He has now decided to share what he has learned from pursuing success in homebuilding for more than 25 years. *The Business of Home Building* is a down-to-earth, nuts-and-bolts practical guide for anyone with the entrepreneurial "fire in the belly" wishing to create decent, affordable housing in their community. José doesn't mess around with arcane theories or models, but rather lays out how it's done in hard-hitting, straightforward detail. For anyone wishing to enter this industry, this book is what they need. In his well-written, well-organized narrative, José shares step-by-step how to do it and be successful at it. If this were an Amazon or Goodreads review, I'd give it five stars. Great job, José.

**–Dr. Roger Morefield, Professor of Economics
at the University of St. Thomas**

The industry has books on building. The industry has books on looking at a home through the eyes of the buyer. The industry has how to avoid mistakes when building or buying. What the industry needs and does not have are the chapters of succinct information in one outstanding, easy-to-read, easy-to-understand book on building. This book written by Jose Berlanga, has all of these nuggets! it is the tool you need if you are wanting excellent direction on many facets of becoming a home builder. I recommend this book be added to not only a want-to-be builder's library but also for real estate professionals who desire more insight into home building.

–**Rita D. Santamaria, owner, founder,
Champions School of Real Estate LTD.**

The Business of Homebuilding is a great read! This book details the potential success and failures of being a homebuilder. Berlanga shares personal experiences that helped identify professional development opportunities for his company, including a step-by-step guide into what to expect when building homes. From land acquisition to securing funding, from construction to sales, the book provides potential entrepreneurs with the necessary tools for success in the homebuilding industry.

–**Rudy Moreno, executive director, City of Houston**

Jose Berlanga unselfishly offers the keys to the kingdom; A way out for someone who is stuck in a rote job who doesn't have access to a new career path. In his book, he offers a candid roadmap to becoming a home builder. Every aspect of this complicated process is explained beautifully in *The Business of Home Building*. I grew up in a household of a home builder. My father built homes for 55 years and what he learned in a lifetime Jose explains succinctly and anecdotally in this valuable read. This book is a must-read for those that want to avoid the pitfalls of an otherwise rewarding industry. Bravo to Berlanga.

–**Charles H. Mansour, BS, JD, LLM in Taxation,
top closing attorney, Fidelity National Title**

Jose Berlanga's *The Business of Home Building* is a masterclass in real estate development. As someone who has successfully built home communities for years, Berlanga offers invaluable insights into entering and prospering in the home-building business. His candid sharing of personal mistakes provides a rare opportunity to learn from someone else's vast experiences, helping readers avoid common pitfalls. This book isn't just about the basics; it delves into recognizing opportunities and thriving in the competitive world of home-building real estate. Whether you're a newbie or seasoned professional, this book is an essential guide for anyone looking to make their mark in home building.

> **–John MacGregor, international best-selling author, keynote speaker, wealth coach personal advisor to Robert Kiyosaki – *Rich Dad Poor Dad***

As a professor of economics and finance, not being in the home-building business, I find the book very well-written, highly engaging, and quite informative. I am certain that this book will prove of great interest to all those active in this industry.

> **–Dr. H. Shirvani, University of St. Thomas**

For anyone considering starting their own home-building company, or even considering a career in the business, Mr. Berlanga's book is a must-read. His book takes a careful, step-by-step approach into all aspects of the business, and most importantly does so in a very easy-to-read manner. The book is insightful and does a great job of explaining some of the pitfalls that many start up home-building companies run into. Navigating the business around these pitfalls is crucial in order to be successful, and his book will help you do just that.

> **–David Orlando, former division president, Brighton Homes and K. Hovnanian Homes**

The Business of Home Building by Jose Berlanga is an essential guide, rich with wisdom from decades of experience in the home-building business. It offers invaluable insights and practical advice, making it a must-read for both newcomers and seasoned professionals seeking to navigate and succeed in this complex field.

–Joanne McCall, owner of McCall Media Group

THE BUSINESS OF
HOME
BUILDING

JOSE M. BERLANGA

Copyright © 2024 Jose M. Berlanga.

All Rights Reserved. This book contains material protected under International and Federal Copyright Laws and Treaties. Any unauthorized reprint or use of this material is prohibited. No part of this book may be reproduced or transmitted in any form or by any means, electronic or mechanical, including photocopying, recording, or by any information storage and retrieval system without express written permission from the author/publisher.

Author is not a financial advisor, realtor, attorney, or CPA.
Consult a qualified professional before proceeding.

print ISBN: 979-8-88636-038-7
ebook ISBN: 979-8-88636-039-4

BUS000000 **BUSINESS & ECONOMICS** / General
BUS054010 **BUSINESS & ECONOMICS** / Real Estate / Buying & Selling Homes
DES009000 **DESIGN** / Industrial

Table of Contents

Introduction 1
Chapter 1   Why Home Building? 13
Chapter 2   Setting Up Your Company. 33
Chapter 3   Surround Yourself with the Right Team 52
Chapter 4   Your First Property or Real Estate Deal 72
Chapter 5   Financial Projections and Home Selections 92
Chapter 6   Budgets—Finding Money and Allocating It 103
Chapter 7   Land Development, Construction Process, and Management. 122
Chapter 8   Financial Management and Market Conditions. . . . 139
Chapter 9   Avoiding Costly Mistakes 155
Chapter 10   Pricing Properties 173
Chapter 11   Marketing Basics 196
Chapter 12   After the Sale. 215
Chapter 13   Conclusion 226

Introduction

Despite all my success as the founder and CEO of several home building-related ventures, I actually never intended to be a builder. It wasn't necessarily my dream. Even after I started building homes, I anticipated only sticking around, at most, a handful of years. I certainly never planned to spend most of my career doing this. Yet here I am, after thirty-five years as an entrepreneur, twenty-five of them dedicated to building close to 2,000 homes, and God knows how many more real estate transactions, having made (and lost) millions. To some, this number of homes may not even seem that large compared to those publicly held companies that produce that amount in less than a year. But for a privately held, inner-city builder with no previous experience, developing small, scattered projects, it's a world of volume that required decades and an endless number of headaches to achieve.

The reason that smaller builders generally produce fewer homes per year than real estate conglomerates is that the level of involvement required in each and every single home is much higher. You are building and redeveloping in already established communities, surrounded by minefields that constantly present new situations, as opposed to having open space with no preexisting conditions to worry about. For example, just to locate and select one piece of land on which to build a couple of homes, first you have to look and drive by probably ten or twenty of them. Then you have to beat the monster competition flooding every neighborhood, which in itself is a challenge. Next, you need to go through your typical development process, consisting of a number of intricate steps. Then you negotiate the deal, perform a careful laundry list of "due diligence" tasks on the land, followed by creating designs, plans, site plans, elevations, permits, surveys, rejections, revisions, restrictions, title work, engineering, encroachments, easements, rights of way, and setbacks. Along the way you have to deal with homeowner associations, architectural committees, the city planning department, utilities, proposals, budgets, projections, estimates, banks, marketing materials, meetings after meetings, and so on. Compared to a tract home builder that can buy a few hundred of these already developed, shovel-ready lots in one single purchase, there is so much more to be done!

Is this passion or an addiction, I have to wonder? After retiring and winding down Tricon Homes, the company I ran with my brother Tristan for more than twenty profitable years and grew to $100 million a year, I've again started investing in another group of residential construction enterprises. At Tricon, we hired hundreds of employees and contractors, worked with more than forty lenders to finance our projects, and survived several decades through multiple economic cycles, downturns, market fluctuations, a major housing bubble, and a world financial crisis that almost took down the entire US economy. Unlike other builders, we never shut down and restarted under a different name to hide our past. We were Tricon Homes for as long as we were actively building, during good years and bad.

Today, I'm still in the home building business, but as an investor/serial entrepreneur, I'm also involved in several other ventures. That has always been the case for me.

Destined to be an entrepreneur

I've been an entrepreneur since I can remember. I was always one of those kids who was constantly looking for ways to make money. By the time I was in high school I had amassed some savings, and the day after my high school graduation, I moved to Houston. I was seventeen and I started my first company, which exported machinery for the petrochemical, oil, and gas business. That's the industry my dad was in. He showed me the ropes and introduced me to his network to help me get my first business off the ground. After earning my first commission payment, I confirmed my love of entrepreneurship. I simply couldn't imagine working for a paycheck—meaning for someone else—and I never have.

That fall I started at the University of St. Thomas, in Houston, studying business administration, economics, and philosophy, all the while continuing to run my businesses. I wasn't thrilled about school, but I knew I wanted to get my degree, so I rushed through it just to get my diploma. My passion was learning about business, which was both a blessing and a curse. It was a blessing because my curiosity led me to increase my knowledge of starting and running businesses, but a curse because I was attracted to *all* the businesses. As opportunities were presented to me, I pursued them if they intrigued me. My focus remained on my core exporting business, but I did dabble in other markets and industries. I've always wanted to own a portfolio of companies; that has been my long-term goal.

During my career, I have been involved in a dozen different industries: valves and piping, manufacturing, telecommunications, advertising, technology, clothing, chemicals, retail, food production, industrial tires, commercial real estate, corporate travel, paper and paper exporting for the label industry, the auto industry, the ice cream business, coffee shops, restaurants, bars, nightclubs, oil & gas, and the list goes on. There were probably a couple dozen businesses that I either operated, participated in, or of which I was on the periphery. However, it was the growth of my exporting business that made me wealthy by age twenty-one.

After doing so well at such a young age, I thought I would retire early and never have to worry about money again. In fact, I enjoyed the business world so much that my plan was to simply own businesses for fun, but never again for necessity. Of course, life had different plans for me. Soon enough the Latin American economy hit a speed bump and my business collapsed; my clients started delaying payments then defaulting, projects came to a halt, and my income went from sixty to zero in a matter of months. In retrospect, at that point I should have cashed out rather than attempt turning things around, when there was no way my business could influence major economic trends. Unfortunately, my inexperience betrayed me and I lost everything.

However, by the time I got into the home building industry, having had my hand in a number of other businesses, I had witnessed turbulent cycles and this knowledge came in handy. I became accustomed to, or at least more comfortable with, dramatic ebbs and flows. That level of comfort and familiarity with market changes is what perhaps allowed me to navigate the murky waters of the real estate world. I had developed an ability to manage companies that were under financial pressure and had limited resources.

Interestingly enough, I think I already had this in my blood. My parents had a great ability to quickly adjust; they knew how to live lavishly when times were good and to become extremely frugal when necessary. My father had a similar trajectory of feast or famine. As a child, I remember my mother becoming very creative and inventing amazing dishes with the few leftovers she found in the refrigerator when we had run out of money and were waiting for my father's next paycheck. I learned at an early age that almost anyone can run a thriving business but not many can run an undercapitalized troubled company and turn it into a success. I tell myself that I am an expert in managing poverty!

A New Partnership

My brother Tristan was the reason I got into the home building business and the inspiration for our company. From a very young age, Tristan was fascinated with designing and constructing things. It was his passion. Everyone around him could see he was destined to be a successful builder and architect. As young boys, he and I envisioned starting our own home building company together. Being partners became one of our life dreams.

Six years my junior, Tristan and I were always very close, protecting, supporting, and encouraging each other throughout our childhood. I wanted this business more for him than for myself, honestly. I wanted to make money but, to me, it really didn't matter in what industry.

Through the years, we refined our business plan. We decided that Tristan would be the home designer and project manager and I would be the behind-the-scenes administrator. Initially, I was not fully involved. My role was helping to set up the business, the finances, and to grow the company. But little by little, as we began to learn the needs and demands of the industry, I became more involved until we were working full-time together.

My original goal was to eventually hand off the day-to-day management to others, once the company was well-established, so that I could get back to what I truly enjoy, which is the start-up process. I love starting new businesses and creating new opportunities, rather than operating them. I also love sharing what I know and what I've learned from others, in the hopes of creating new opportunities for everyone.

Our plan was put into motion soon after Tristan became an architect, graduating from the University of Houston, and while he was working for the city as a plan checker. After spending some time in the job and gaining experience inspecting properties, Tristan approached me about partnering on our first project.

We didn't realize it at that moment, but the timing was perfect to go into business together.

Our first property

Tristan started studying local neighborhoods, checking out contractors, and preparing a list of things that needed to happen to build a house. We didn't know all that was involved because at that point, neither of us had actually built a house on our own.

We were optimists—absolutely sure we would be successful at whatever we put our minds to. After all, how hard could building a house be? Yes, ignorance is bliss. We didn't know all that we didn't know, but we would soon find out.

I funded the start-up company with $7,500. Part of my job description was to act as the investor and to oversee the money aspects, his was to design and build the homes. Those were the company's original two departments: finance and building. Using that initial investment to buy our first lot, we embarked on this journey.

This was in the 1990s, when most neighborhoods with proximity to downtown Houston had been forgotten. As with most large cities, the housing market had grown tremendously, and buyers had fled to the suburbs in search of better value and more land. Which meant there were great opportunities for us. These weren't, however, the most attractive homes. It meant that we would have to build a new house surrounded with teardowns. To get to it, you would have to drive through a rough neighborhood. This was a risky proposition that wasn't proven or popular.

As we drove through neighborhoods in transition to get to the spot where Tristan proposed we build our first house, I grew increasingly concerned. It was a scary drive, even in daylight. And then he pulled over.

"Are you sure this is it?" I asked him. "What are we doing here?" I said, incredulous that he thought this downtrodden area of Houston Heights was a smart place to be then. Turns out, this was where he wanted to build our first house.

Tristan had vision. He had noticed that people were, little by little, starting to recognize what they were missing by being outside the metro area. Buyers were starting to head back into the city, where all the bars, restaurants, and clubs were located. Not to mention, the traffic from the suburbs was becoming absurd. Tristan saw this and predicted that in a matter of years, Houston Heights would be fashionable again. He found a lot and wanted to show me. "This is the place where we can start with very little money and learn the business," he pointed out. It was affordable and also would allow us to build a product at a price point that no one else was offering at the time.

He envisioned that the area would change. However, standing in the street back then, I was not so sure and, frankly, I wasn't convinced. But I believed in him. As it turns out, he was right. The Heights, one of the first residential communities originally developed in the late 1800s, has now been completely revitalized, becoming one of the most sought-after inner-city neighborhoods in Houston. I can comfortably say that we had a lot to do with it. We took a gamble and subsequently built hundreds of new homes in this subdivision, and later in many other transitional neighborhoods, making it attractive for other builders to follow.

Our plan then was to buy the lot for $7,500, build a little one-story, 800- or 900-square-foot bungalow, and sell it for under $100,000 to net a tidy profit. This seemed very reasonable, maybe even conservative, to us at the time. (Today, that same $7,500 lot would sell for around $500,000, just to make clear how right Tristan was.)

Of course, nothing is ever that easy or that profitable at first. We paid cash for the lot but borrowed for the construction. While we were in the middle of building the home, Tristan approached me with good news: "Hey, I sold the house!" he told me.

I was a little confused since the house wasn't done and we hadn't listed it for sale. Yet, he had actually sold it, even unfinished. A buyer had seen what we were creating and wanted it, paying what we had asked for the property. So, we finished and delivered it as promised.

Did we make lots of money on the deal? No, we did not. In fact, we lost a little. But I wasn't bothered by that. As a matter of fact, I was thrilled. I was excited because we had accomplished our goal. We had bought in an unproven market—in what I feared might be an unpopular or even uninhabitable block—and somebody wanted the house we had built. My reaction was, "I think we have something here. Let's keep going!"

The start of something big

We both recognized that we needed to perfect our business process, by reviewing the numbers, our pricing, our expenses—all the components that make up a successful project. To be able to stay in the home building business long-term, we had to carefully calculate not only what it was going to cost money-wise, but what each project would cost in terms of our time. How long a home would take to build emerged as an important consideration as we developed more refined pricing guides for ourselves.

The good news for us was that our skills complemented each other's. Where Tristan was the artist and visionary, I was the administrative and finance partner. In most successful businesses you typically find partners who balance each other skill-wise. Take Steve Jobs and Steve Wozniak at Apple, for example, or Bill Gates and Paul Allen at Microsoft, Larry Page and Sergey Brin of Google, and Ben Cohen and Jerry Greenfield of Ben & Jerry's Ice Cream. Creative people don't necessarily know how to run businesses, and people who know how to manage companies may not necessarily have the technical or innovation knowledge required to keep a business operating. Rarely can one person do it all.

Tristan and I worked well together, starting with that first house.

That was a big leap of faith for us. We were risking our money and our time in the hopes that we could build a property that someone would want to buy. That is the essence of being an entrepreneur, isn't it? You put your money in, invest lots of time and hard work, you even take on more debt to get the project done, not getting paid through the process, all in the hope that everything you've invested will return to you. However, somewhere along the way you realize that now you're either going to lose your time or your money, or if you get lucky and make money, it will all have to be reinvested in the next project. From the outside looking in, entrepreneurship sounds exciting and liberating, but once you're in it, it can be more like insanity if you don't have what it takes.

But we didn't start this particular business with big plans to become millionaires. Our dream to work side-by-side came to fruition because of Tristan's keen attention to what was going on in the housing market. And despite the fact that we knew so little about how it actually worked, we succeeded over time, frequently through trial and error. You have the advantage of having picked up this book—you'll learn from our mistakes, as well as some of the things we should have thought about prior to getting started, plus, of course, a few of the smart decisions we did make along the way.

The fact is most people have an unrealistic view of how home building works. It sounds much easier than it is. Part of the problem is the proliferation of home building, home design, and home décor TV shows that share only part of the process. They don't broadcast the tedious engineering calculations, material estimating, and back-breaking work that happens behind the scenes long before paint colors are selected and finishes are installed. I really think the complexity of this industry is underrated and underappreciated. The personality type and amount of knowledge required to be successful goes far beyond what most people expect. Yet everyone thinks they can do it.

Unfortunately, those who jump in without a background in the field soon find themselves in over their heads. It's easy to get into that situation. It is well-documented that this particular business causes anxiety, stress, frustration, insomnia, financial hardship, personal conflicts, and even marital issues. I've seen many people who are way more educated than I am get into home building and then quickly leave, either because they got kicked out or because they went broke. Many businesses have come and gone because they presumed home building was as fun and easy as HGTV or The Magnolia Network makes it look. And it's not.

Theoretically, anyone can do it. Yes, if you have carte blanche to spend whatever is necessary and no deadline, sure, you can be successful. But as soon as you have restrictions, either financial, or governmental, or schedule-wise, things get tough very quickly.

Think about it. Would you ever attempt to build your own car in thirty days? I don't know many people who would try, given all the US Department of Transportation rules and regulations, as well as guidelines from the National Highway Traffic Safety Administration, the US Environmental Protection Agency, the Clean Air Act, not to mention the engineering expertise required to even get started, regardless of the deadline. Declaring that you're going to build your own vehicle without at least being a mechanic would sound ridiculous to most people, because the design and production process is so complex. Although a much pricier and riskier undertaking, somehow this logic does not seem to apply to home building and I think it should.

That level of complexity also exists for houses, though few people realize the extent of federal and local regulations that must be followed in order for a structure to be raised. You have to coordinate hundreds of details and numerous steps, receive approval from multiple entities, and work with inconsistent variables and terrains. Then you have to connect existing infrastructures and services to new ones, like private and public streets, water, sewer, electrical, gas, cable, and fire department. To build a house, it will have to meet a long list of requirements with confusing interpretations and opinions from dozens of participants, all the while ensuring that everything passes a series of inspections that adhere to each individual agency's demands. And this is just a partial list. The process is intricate and complicated, to say the least.

Now that you may be second-guessing your interest in getting into home building, let me reassure you that even though you may not know everything right now, no one becomes an expert in a single step. I'm going to talk you through some of the most important steps in this process, so that you can better understand what the most common sequence of events is.

In the coming chapters, you're going to learn the A to Z of starting a home building business. I won't be teaching you the ins and outs of construction, however, because that's beyond the scope of this book. There are already plenty of manuals and videos for that purpose. What I'll share with you is more about establishing and managing the business aspects of a profitable home building enterprise, which are often ignored.

What you'll learn

Now that my home building business experience has evolved, I thought it was the perfect time to write this book—to create new opportunities for others, like you, who are contemplating getting into home building. Hopefully, I can save you a lot of time, money, frustration, and plenty of despair—which I have certainly experienced—by sharing what I've learned along the way. My hope is that after you read these stories, my perspective on things, why I did what I did and made the choices I made, you can begin to spot the opportunities out there and help you negotiate deals that maximize the upside while reducing your level of risk.

I will share with you basic functions on how to start and how to run a home building business. I will begin with some background information on how the industry works, and the many ways you can opt to get involved. Incidentally, this book can be extremely useful not only for this industry but for any business that you wish to start, since it contains some fundamental and extremely important aspects of the start-up process that can guide you through navigating the logic of building a company.

CHAPTER 1

Why Home Building?

I always enjoy learning the history of different industries—their genealogy, essentially—and found the origins of home building in the US to be equally fascinating.

A little backstory

Part of this story begins with the history of homebuying and consumer trends. Until the 1800s, true home builders weren't popular in the US. People built their own homes when they could afford the materials and the labor, which was rare. In fact, in America the main reason to own land in that period was for farming. But buying land was difficult and expensive. Banks didn't do much lending and mortgages did not yet exist. The only way to buy land, for the average person, was through a for-sale-by-owner arrangement with the previous landowner.

However, the opportunity for land ownership changed dramatically with the passing of the National Banking Act of 1860. Introduced to stabilize the economy, the act also created a system that allowed banks to lend to the average consumer. By 1890, mortgages were almost commonplace, although they were structured nothing like what we have today. They required a large down payment—close to fifty percent—with short repayment periods (a maximum of five years with a balloon payment), and they were complicated to even apply for.

Despite the fact that approval was challenging, because mortgages were a possible way to own land, demand surged. As a result, in 1908 the National Association of Realtors (originally named the National Association of Real Estate) was founded and in 1916, the National Association of Real Estate Boards adopted the word "Realtor" to represent professionals trained to help Americans buy and sell properties.

In 1956, the entire homeownership landscape changed with the kick-off of the interstate highway system. New roads and highways made it possible for employees to live outside the inner city and led to an explosion of tract homes being built in planned communities. Construction companies grew exponentially to keep up with demand.

> The first master-planned community was built during the 1940s in Levittown, New York, and consisted of about 17,000 homes on 6,000 acres. Builders used techniques adopted straight from the assembly lines of the automotive industry, which enabled them to complete anywhere from thirty to thirty-five homes in a day. This role model community and the home building techniques used there forever changed the housing industry.

This pushed the home building industry out of the inner city, which had little land left on which to build, and into the suburbs. Which meant that from the 1960s into the late 1980s, downtown areas and the rings around them were all but forgotten. In many cities, they became low-income areas. All the residential activity was focused outside the city limits, because it was much easier for real estate developers to buy large plots of land and build homes by the hundreds or thousands. The economies of scale there spelled profit, whereas the inner city, with its limited available land, was of less interest to large builders. Everyone wanted to live in the suburbs until the late 1980s, when the tide turned and people began to consider moving closer in, rather than farther away. By the 1990s, living in downtown areas started to become downright cool again for many cities. Smaller builders began buying up individual lots or properties in disrepair to either renovate and revitalize them or to tear them down and rebuild on them.

This is where we come in, the point at which Tristan and I started looking for properties in and around downtown Houston, not aware at the time that we were part of this larger redevelopment trend. We were among the smaller builders who knew we couldn't compete with the mammoth builders in the suburbs, so we stayed focused on the scattered individual homes that had been neglected or run down, where we had less competition. Fortunately, we were on the leading edge of that shift back into the city limits, which led to many years of success in refurbishing or redeveloping homes that had been all but forgotten.

The industry

With an average of one million new homes built each year by approximately 400,000 registered home builders, the bulk of them being smaller firms, there is clearly plenty of opportunity in this industry.

Although it's very possible to do well in home building, I wouldn't necessarily tell you that it is easy. It is, however, a great industry to join as an entrepreneur, because home building will expose you to many aspects of the world of business. You'll see the hands-on, physical work involved in creating something tangible from scratch, as well as experiencing economics up close. You'll gain familiarity with how financial markets work, as well as how sales strategies and psychology can be applied, on top of accounting, negotiation, purchasing, marketing, technology, legal—you name it! Home building brings together virtually every aspect of running a business, giving you the opportunity to become an extremely well-rounded businessperson after only a few years in this field. The skills you'll develop are so diverse that you'll be able to apply them to nearly any other type of business if you decide that home building isn't where you belong.

For example, if you're a creative person, through home building you can learn about the design and architecture aspects of home construction. Or you may apply your talents to marketing and perfect your graphic design or social media skills. You can strengthen your computer skills, learn about décor, interior design, and/or website creation, finance, engineering, or management. And if you decide that the home building business isn't for you, all of the expertise and abilities you'll gain will be applicable elsewhere—this isn't such a niche business that you won't be able to use what you've learned in another field.

As I've told you, I never intended to make home building my life. This was supposed to be one more step in my career, but little by little, the industry became part of my blood. For one reason or another, once I got involved, I was hooked. There was always so much to do, so much to learn, so much to create and improve that there was no time to consider walking away from it. It was sort of like playing sports where the better you become, the more you get involved, and the moment you get it right and actually generate a profit, you find it difficult to stop. Even if you don't make money on every deal, your mind convinces you that you have a chance. The business has a gambling aspect to it because, if you think about it, every single project is an entirely new deal. Also, the project cycles are long, so by default, the nature of the business gets you emotionally involved. Every deal makes it harder to drop the industry for greener pastures. Like a personal relationship, the more years you invest in it, the more meaningful it becomes and the harder it gets to walk away.

Unlike many other professions where you receive regular payments or daily performance updates, whether you own a restaurant, pharmacy, boutique, hair salon, repair shop, gas station, bakery, or medical facility, you can get regular feedback in the form of sales. In the residential construction business, with every transaction, the anticipation and waiting period is long. When, finally, one single moment when your home sells determines whether the last couple of years of your life's work made sense or not. Then, following the closure of that cycle, you turn around to start the process all over again, with the success of one project not guaranteeing the success of the next. Every deal gives you a lot to think about.

I think part of the reason so many people are drawn to home building and real estate is that land is a finite commodity (they're not making any more of it, after all), which is why real estate is such a huge portion of the investment landscape. Real estate is tangible (you can touch it), it has proven to be a smart hedge against inflation, values have consistently increased, and perhaps an even bigger factor is that as humans, we have an emotional connection to our homes. Real estate represents safety and security, as well as serving as a source of personal pride. Your home is the biggest investment you'll probably ever make. It's a symbol of freedom, wealth, and success. It's your own little kingdom.

Interestingly, once you buy a house, that building becomes a home. The simple act of you owning it changes its meaning. There is no other product that is like that, where you purchase a physical product, and it transitions from one thing to another, from a house to a home. It becomes part of your life and your identity. It's where you spend much of your time, where you create memories. Your home often tells a story of who you are.

Is this business for you?

We've already established that homes are central to our sense of self, that investors have trillions of dollars wrapped up in the construction, development, management, and sale of homes, and that many people want to be part of the game. It's a fast-paced industry where big money has been made and lost.

However, all of that is immaterial. You need to decide for yourself if home building is the right business *for you*. Just because it worked well for me and for others does not necessarily mean that it's the ideal type of business for you. Of course, some of the biggest plusses of this business include:

- You're able to grow as much or as little as you want—you're in control
- You own and run your life, your schedules, and your systems
- You never stop learning, since the business is ever-changing and evolving
- It has a mix of indoor and outdoor work
- There is plenty of hands-on physical work to be done
- The barrier to entry is relatively small
- You don't need a lot of training or a college degree
- Yes, you can make a lot of money

For many new business owners, perhaps the biggest advantage of leaving full-time employment is that you can be your own boss. You can be totally in control of your schedule, your earning potential, and the work that you take on. But you also need to realize that you're leaving one boss and getting multiple bosses in return, because each one of your clients, lenders, and investors is a boss. In many ways, you don't own your business, but your business owns you, because you will constantly be thinking about it. At least, those who are successful become fully immersed in it.

Some of the cons or disadvantages include:

- Long hours. This is not a 9:00 to 5:00 job but more like 7:00 a.m. to 7:00 p.m. on a good day, typically six days a week (seven if you have buyers or homes on the market)

- The need to be present—be on-site—for things to happen as they should
- Staying current on rules, regulations, local codes, the competition
- Many activities and subcontractors to manage; you must be a multitasker who can't afford to spend too much time on one subject
- Because the barrier to entry is relatively small, there is more unstable competition
- You won't get a regular paycheck. You may not get paid until the entire project is completed
- It is capital intensive. When you do start making money, most of it needs to be reinvested in order to grow
- The business is feast or famine and hard to predict; you must have high tolerance to risk

Setting aside funds for added contingencies—unexpected situations that end up costing you extra money—is a smart move. This money you've set aside will help keep you afloat if you end up having to pay two electricians because the first one walked out mid-project, or you had to replace a painter and the new one costs more, or if it takes longer to sell the house you've just built than you anticipated. You need to stockpile cash for as long as possible. If you can't build the house without paying yourself during the process, it's better not to start. This is a business, not a job. You get paid when the house gets sold; you don't get paid in advance, not as a business owner anyway.

Many new home builders recognize that they'll have to sacrifice a few years learning the business inside and out. However, the truth is, not everyone in this industry is all-in; some participants are not even full-time, not passionate enough or fully devoted. This is often their side business or just something they got into expecting to make easy money. This business requires hard work and not everyone is willing to do it, which gives you an advantage.

Choose from among several business models

I want to recommend that you stay away from full restoration projects, which involve taking all the walls of a building down to the studs and replacing mechanical, electrical, and plumbing systems for the purpose of maintaining the shell of the original exterior look of the house. This requires dealing with numerous surprises that can emerge inside and under an old structure. This process is not to be confused with remodeling or with flipping homes, which is considerably easier and mostly cosmetic. There are a sequence of uncertainties and surprises that will just continue to show up on these types of projects, making the cost estimating a total guess. There are many rules and regulations and unnecessary maneuvering only justified if a house has true historic or architectural value. Unless you are an expert in this field, I would not attempt it. What you thought was going to take a couple of months might end up taking a couple of years and be a financial disaster.

What's exciting about the real estate industry is that there are so many facets to it. There are multiple ways to become part of this field, as well as multiple markets, from residential to commercial, industrial, healthcare, retail, and agricultural, to name just a few categories of projects. There are also a number of different roles that can be played without starting a home building company, including surveyors, appraisers, inspectors, soil report engineers, architects, and designers, just to name a few. There are also skilled tradespeople, such as plumbers, electricians, carpenters, framers, drywallers, masons, HVAC contractors, and many others who make essential contributions to the construction of a home. These various roles are part of the home building process—they are all pieces of the home building puzzle.

There are different ways to get into or participate in the home building business, which I'm going to refer to as business models. Different business models operate in different ways and serve different parts of the industry. Some examples of the most common business models include:

- **Technical.** Serving as a subcontractor to address one single aspect of the home building process, such as framing, demolition, plumbing, or carpentry. This type of business is frequently a small entity, owned and operated by the founder and can be very profitable. This approach is highly technical and specialized in whatever area you choose.
- **Remodeling & Additions.** In my opinion, quick remodeling is one of the best models for entering the business. Remodeling occurs when a homeowner hires you to update parts of the house they bought by changing cosmetic components. That can include, for example, swapping out the kitchen countertops and cabinets, redoing bathroom tile or hardwood floors, cleaning up the landscaping, or even removing a non-load-bearing wall to make the space seem larger. Remodeling is focused on improving appearance within a home that is already owned. **Additions** involve adding a new structure to an old one and being skilled enough to be able to merge the two seamlessly, from flooring to the roof to the heat and air conditioning. The homeowner might add a porch or decide to extend the whole house, top to bottom, on one side and the trick is to avoid making the transition obvious.
- **Flipping.** Flipping is a different business model because instead of working as a vendor for a homeowner, you actually buy a house and renovate it with the intent to resell it to a different buyer for a profit. You are both the client and the supplier in this case, which requires you to invest and borrow money to get started.
- **General contractor.** This model involves building a house for someone else, assuming responsibility for coordinating all aspects of the construction process. Overseeing the build

and being able to bill the owner for every step in the process is lower risk than other approaches. A general contractor often bills the client on a cost-plus basis. The contractor takes no responsibility for overages, however, and merely passes them along to the homeowner to pay.

+ **Turnkey general contractor.** While the services provided by a turnkey contractor mirror that of a general contractor, the main difference is that a turnkey contractor quotes a price to build a home on a per-square-foot basis, which is much riskier. The client hands over a full set of architectural plans, specifications, permits, permitted plans, finishes, and selections and the turnkey general contractor quotes a set price based on the size and details of the house. For example, at $300/square foot, a 2,000-square-foot home would cost the customer $600,000 to build through this type of contractor. However, the turnkey contractor has assumed all of the risk associated with pricing and if prices are not locked in and happen to skyrocket, their profit could evaporate.

+ **Developer-investor.** Where the contractor completes the work, a developer-investor hires a contractor to execute the construction and focuses on the business side of the house. They have access to money and put deals together, rather than actually swinging a hammer. Also called a "builder developer," this type of participant works to keep the business afloat and profitable without actually doing the hands-on work.

+ **Passive investor.** A developer-investor is an active investor who helps manage the financial side of the business, while a passive investor funds the deal and nothing more. Using a trusted and experienced team, the passive investor provides equity capital to fund a build, but nothing else, in exchange for receiving a percentage of profits on top of the return of their capital when the house sells. If you try this route, make sure to perform the appropriate due diligence before investing. There are plenty of bad, inexperienced players out there attempting to raise capital.

- **Land developer.** When you buy land, subdivide the lots, replat them (meaning divide them up), permit them, build the infrastructure, and then sell the shovel-ready lots to other builders, you are a land developer. You don't have anything to do with the actual construction of the houses, other than preparing the land on which they will be built. This is not an easy process and risky because your pool of buyers is very limited, but under the right circumstances it can be very profitable.
- **Full-blown builder.** A full-blown builder does everything, from raising or putting up capital, obtaining financing, negotiating, to finding the land, identifying contractors, supervising them through the process, securing all the raw materials needed, managing the project and the financial accounting, retaining a real estate agent to sell it, and then selling it. You do everything associated with the project from start to finish.

The main difference between these various business models is the amount of involvement and responsibility you take at every step of the process. Depending on whether you want to fund the company's growth, buy up the land, hire subcontractors to handle the construction, and sell the property, or whether you want to specialize in one piece of that process determines the extent of your involvement and liability. Only you can decide how large a role you want to play in the home building process.

But understand that you do not need to go out and hire dozens of workers to be able to operate as a builder. Starting out, you'll want to rely on independent contractors, or workers who are not employees and who are hired to complete specific pieces of the job. You can subcontract, or farm out, everything from demolition to cabinetry, dry wall, roofing, etc. You do not have to become an expert in every individual step and do it yourself, nor do you have to hire employees to get the work done. Start small and grow from there.

To outsource or hire?

Generally, most of the work in this industry is outsourced to contractors who are skilled at their particular craft. From foundation to framing, roofing, electrical, plumbing, or finishes, you don't need to employ someone full-time when you only need that kind of help on a case-by-case basis. You pay only for the work being done.

When you're just starting out and trying to conserve cash, even the administrative duties are best outsourced or done by yourself, if possible.

However, as your business grows and you find yourself managing multiple projects at once, there will come a time when it makes sense to hire talent on an ongoing basis, rather than when needed. That point generally arrives when you see that you are paying contractors more than you would pay a full-time employee to do any one given duty, but you need to have a steady workload to make it work, which of course comes with a new source of stress.

There are pros and cons to using contractors, just as there are pros and cons to having employees. Here are what I believe to be the biggest advantages and disadvantages of each:

Subcontractors

Pros
- ✦ You pay only for the work you need done.
- ✦ You can tie expenses directly back to a particular house, which helps with accounting.
- ✦ If the market slows down, you are less affected because you're only paying for services as you need them. No need to downsize or to make the painful decision to let employees go.

- If one subcontractor doesn't perform, or doesn't show up, you can explore other options quickly without having wasted time and money training an employee.
- You have more flexibility and can even use multiple companies simultaneously to provide the same service in different projects to try them out.

Cons

- You have less control over their availability, since you are one of several clients.
- You may pay a little more per house for that flexibility.
- It may take longer to get things done if they have too much on their plate, especially from the good ones with high demand.

Employees

Pros

- You have more control over your employees' time and how they spend it on your projects.
- They are always available to work strictly on your projects with complete focus.
- You can shift priorities easily and reassign employees accordingly for the benefit of your company.
- There is more profit potential, since the cost per project can be less than what you would pay subcontractors.

Cons

- You have to pay them whether they work at all or not, or whether you have enough for them to do or not.
- You need to manage their time and ensure their productivity and offer bonus plans and incentives to create a sense of urgency.
- Your overhead becomes less predictable, because if things fall behind for issues beyond your employees' control, like

- changes in code or bad weather, they continue to get paid even as your projects are, for whatever reason, put on hold.
- The more employees you add to your overhead, the more you have to produce each month to be able to afford them, forcing you to take on projects whether you want to or not.

The workforce you need to build houses falls on a spectrum, really, with independent contractors on one end and employees on the other. You can start out 100 percent outsourced to contractors and then gradually shift some of that work onto employees. But when you're building one or two houses a year, it's unlikely you'll need employees. It just doesn't make sense to have such high overhead at the start.

I will admit that it can be tough to determine whether it makes sense to hire employees, or at what point. During strong years, you may not figure out your optimal head count until things hit a rough patch. When Tricon was growing steadily in the early 2000s, every house that we built we would immediately sell. So, it seemed to me, every house that we couldn't build was costing us money. Let's pretend we were earning $50,000 per house, just to keep the math easy, and our inability to build more quickly was effectively limiting our revenue potential. Which pushed us to bring on employees left and right in order to increase our capacity to build more houses. We hired more superintendents, more bookkeepers, more architects—you name it, we were expanding those departments. And while we were building homes, everything was fine. The more people working on our behalf, the faster we could build, and the more money we could bring in, so I wasn't all that concerned with how many employees we actually had. I might even have lost count at one point.

Until the recession hit in 2008. When everything came crashing down, we had to stop and take stock of who on our staff was essential to the company. We had to evaluate the impact that each department, each employee, was having on our bottom line. And we discovered that instead of the fifty or so people on our payroll, we could build just as many houses with, say, thirty. That is the downside of employees—you really don't always know who's helping you be profitable and who is costing you money.

We started out relying on subcontractors to get our work done and began hiring employees only when we reached a point where we needed access to certain skills on a regular basis. Eventually, our company grew to $400,000 or so in monthly overhead. That was $400,000 my brother and I had to pay every month whether we made any money or not. That was in addition to the interest/carrying cost to support our work in progress, translating to $1 million a month to stay in business, sales or no sales. That obligation was pressure that kept us moving forward in order to be able to afford the payments. Of course, the amount of stress, time, and money that it took to create that infrastructure, perhaps decades to get to this point, made it difficult to dismantle even as it became absolutely necessary.

When things get tough, your emotions, fear, ego, and greed kick in, and you go into denial. The pressure confuses you and blurs your thoughts, interfering with your ability to make tough decisions, like to immediately stop building when it's clearly in your best interest to do so. It becomes incredibly difficult to accept the fact that it's time to not take on any new projects, so, as they say, you "continue to feed the monster."

Somehow we survived, with a much lighter staff and, as a result, moved back to outsourcing some of the services that we had previously brought in-house. We had employees in our land acquisitions department, sales, marketing, IT, purchasing, accounting, design, engineering, project superintendents, warranty, even human resources at one point to help us expedite the process of hiring. Nearly everything was in-house because we were working on so many houses simultaneously. And these weren't cookie cutter suburban tract homes, but the inner-city scattered projects with an endless number of different floor plans, styles, elevations, finishes, and price points, all in a dozen different neighborhoods. That meant we were dealing with multiple homeowner associations, architectural committees, city inspectors, flood zones, and soils—always dealing with angry neighbors and demanding buyers. The only thing not in-house were the construction crews building the houses. In fact, even the largest builders don't generally have those skilled trades on their payroll.

The value of specialization

I'm sure you've heard the adage that "you can't be all things to all people." Or, "try to serve everyone and you'll serve no one." Those often-repeated phrases are the essence of why choosing to be a specialist when you're just starting out in home building makes a lot of sense. Trying to be a generalist will be more expensive, more time-consuming, and make it more challenging to establish a name for yourself.

Just as there are many different types of restaurants, from Asian to Mexican, Italian, steakhouses, or all-you-can-eat buffets, there are also different types of homebuilders. The type of homebuilder you may decide to be will likely vary by:

- **Geography.** Where do you currently live, or where have you previously lived? You'll want to start in a locale you're familiar with. Don't start in a town you've never lived in or that is far from you.
- **Price point.** Are you building entry-level homes or mansions?
- **Area.** Will you be building in the inner city or in the suburbs?
- **Format.** Will you be building single-family homes, patio homes, or multifamily?
- **Style.** Will you be building modern houses, Tudor-style, Victorian, or farm-style homes?
- **Buyer.** Will you be targeting young families, single professionals, or retirees?

Not sure how to decide? It's always smart to fall back on what you know, or what interests you. What types of projects do you have experience with? What type of client do you prefer serving? Where do you want to be operating? These answers can help point you to the type of house you may want to specialize in.

Choosing a neighborhood

Before you go all-in, however, spend some time researching your top three areas or neighborhoods, to be sure there is enough demand there for you to be able to make money in it. You can do this by looking at:

+ How many houses are currently on the market?
+ How many houses have sold in the last six months to a year?
+ How many are currently pending?

Then do some calculations. Based on those numbers, how many houses are selling each month? How quickly are they selling? If you find that three homes sold in the last year and there are currently six on the market, that means you currently have a two-year inventory. That may not be a good place to start. But if twenty houses sold in the last six months and there are currently three available,

I recommend not trying to build a house at a price point you've never lived in. Let's say you want to build a $600,000 house, but you've never lived in a house worth more than, say, $300,000. Or, on the flip side, you've only lived in million-dollar mansions and you want to try your hand at $250,000 entry-level homes. That's not a good idea. You won't truly understand what a buyer at that price point wants and expects. You don't know their lifestyle, the amenities they're used to, or their priorities, which would make it very difficult to build a house for a market you aren't familiar with and make money.

that's a good market to be in. The number of homes sold in the last six months to a year is a great gauge of demand for houses in that area.

A healthy, or balanced, market is one that is neither a buyer's market nor a seller's market. That happens when there is approximately a six-month supply of houses available. When there are too few or too many houses available, one party wields more power than the other, and that's not balanced.

Once you decide what type of house to specialize in, stick with it until you master it. Moving around to areas that you think have higher demand or deciding to change the type of home you build will only prolong your struggle for success.

All markets are good. All markets are bad. It all comes down to execution, and moving around is not going to make you a better builder. Pick one, stick with it, and become good at it before expanding into new areas.

Defining your company's mission and vision

Now that you've zeroed in on the type of house you want to build and the type of customer you want to serve, it's time to create a mission and vision statement for your company.

A mission statement is a way for you to describe your company's competitive advantage. What makes you better and different from other builders? What type of experience are you hoping to give your buyer? Why did you choose to build that type of home or to work in that particular area? How are you hoping to impact your customers' lives for the better? Weave in a sense of why you do what you do.

Obviously, we all want to be the best. We want to grow. We want to make money. We want to be successful, but what is your special sauce? What problem are you solving that no one else is?

At Tricon, we recognized in our early years that many houses in Houston were being constructed in the suburbs but seemed to

WHY HOME BUILDING?

lack luxury features in relation to the price. They were more about space than quality of finishes, so we began building in transitional neighborhoods where our mission was to provide real value. The most home for your money was our goal, in the sense that all the cool upgraded finishes were standard at no additional price, which became our unofficial tag line. We compromised a bit on the profit to give buyers more luxury features than the competition for a lower price just to gain recognition. Then we witnessed home values slowly increase as we beautified the neighborhood. Home values rapidly went up, constantly making money for our buyers, and those outside the neighborhood started to notice the transition, which made us popular for not only building a great home but for selling a great investment.

> "House hacking" has become a common strategy for home builders to be able to afford to acquire, renovate, and then resell an updated home for a profit. Essentially, house hacking requires that you buy a property to build or to flip, which you live in or rent for at least two years after you complete the construction or while the renovations and updating are occurring. That way, you buy at builder's cost and when you sell it after two years, you have no income tax or capital gains on the profit, since single owners have up to a $250,000 exclusion and married couples a $500,000 exclusion, making this a tax-free benefit.

So, your mission is what you stand for and your vision statement is how you see your business growing and thriving. It's an inspirational statement designed to help those around you picture where your company is headed in the next five to ten years. It's your future picture of your company.

This exercise of crafting a mission and vision statement is important early on because entrepreneurs frequently act on emotion more than logic. They make decisions based on gut feeling as they proceed without a clear plan of attack. But having these statements to guide decision-making helps ensure that the company is moving toward your ultimate goal, and that it is serving the customers you're targeting in the way that you intended to.

As humans, owning a home is an important process. We aren't considered financially successful or stable until we buy a home. Moving from an apartment to a home you have a mortgage on signals your rising success to those around you. It is a source of pride. Most people want to be part of the American Dream, to be able to own, rather than rent, the place where they live. Owning your own space is fulfilling and rewarding and is why many builders are drawn to the industry—to be part of a process that provides such joy and fulfillment to the buyer.

CHAPTER 2

Setting Up Your Company

Life is filled with responsibilities and never-ending to-do lists, so it may feel like there is never a perfect time to start something new, whether we're talking about taking a long vacation, learning a new hobby, going back to school, having children, or starting a business. You will always have conflicting priorities to juggle and choices to make, some significant and others inconsequential. And it can be hard to distinguish one from the other—the important from the trivial. Therefore, let's just accept that there is rarely a perfect time to start a business, and if you wait for it, it may never come. A lot has to do with destiny and with having a little bit of luck on your side. After all, as they say, timing is everything. But the thing about timing is that you normally don't know if you chose well until much, much later.

We are all born with certain instincts and desires, and they kick in at different moments in time. For some people, owning a business may be on their bucket list. The first step to pursuing those desires is to recognize it, and the second step is to act on it, without worrying too much about regret or the other paths not taken.

Years from now, the regret of not doing what you really want to do, or pursuing this dream you have, will grow larger than the scary feeling of the unknown that you are currently experiencing. So, the answer to when is the best time to start your own business is *now*.

Life will only get busier and there will always be obstacles. You only live once and it's not worth wasting this precious journey doing something that you hate. The big question is what would you love to be doing if you had the choice?

Whether you have your entire career ahead of you or you find yourself mentally drained and unfulfilled with your current one, just know that you can always choose to make a change starting today. No matter what else is going on in your life, whether that's in a new job, a new company, or a new industry, where you've been doesn't necessarily determine where you're headed. You can always decide to do something different. Your life belongs to you!

However, realistically speaking, there are a few things to weigh before moving forward that could improve your chances of success, now or in the future. When you're on the outside of the business world looking in, wondering if now is the right time for you to start building homes, there are two factors to consider: 1) Is it a good time market-wise and 2) Is it a good time for you personally?

Is now the right time?

Market-wise, the real estate industry is cyclical and unpredictable. What that means is that there are extreme highs and lows. So, let's say that the market is booming, as it was when we came out of the worst of the pandemic. Buyers had cash-in-hand, and they were wanting more space and were willing to pay a premium for it. With so many buyers, maybe you assumed that was the best time to get in, because homes were selling rapidly for inflated prices. However, the reality was that because the market was booming, lots of new real estate players—from agents to builders to subcontractors—flooded the market. Newer builders found it hard to stand out and establish a competitive advantage. Unless you were already well-positioned, despite all the demand, success was short-lived.

During a booming market, more new companies are likely to jump in, thinking that there are so many opportunities that they can't lose. Not so. Staying in business comes with very different challenges, because setting up shop in this industry and having a construction site ready to break ground doesn't happen overnight. By the time you are ready to pour your first foundation, who knows what the market will be like? It can change in a matter of weeks. I often say that one of the difficult things about this business is that the decisions I make today will impact my life in a couple of years and only then will I know if I made the right choice. This is not a business where you can simply open your doors and have product to sell the next day. You need vision, discipline, and a lot of forecasting, not last-minute impulse decisions. The markets change so rapidly that you should not base your future on what is happening out there this moment.

On the flip side, during a slow market, it can be hard to make money as a builder, despite not having much competition. When the market is bad, or soft, the industry seems unattractive, and few people think of joining the home building community. They're in defense mode, typically, and taking a risk by starting a new business is uncommon. Interestingly enough, this is the time I would choose.

Although it appears counterintuitive, when the market is slow may actually be a better time to start dabbling in home building. There are better buying opportunities, you're competing with fewer builders, and the ones still around are too busy focusing on how to "stay alive," as opposed to expanding or putting out offers on land deals. As a result, there are more available contractors, better prices, and preferred attention from vendors or service providers. You also have more time to learn the process without being squeezed by everyone. In other words, you need to position yourself, wait patiently, be on your surfboard very attentively, and wait for the right wave, instead of trying to jump on a wave after it's already moving fast; that's actually when most new builders attempt to start.

The state of the market is only one factor to weigh, however, based on my experiences. As with everything else in life, the younger you are the better, because you'll have more time to play with and to compound your knowledge. Although age should not be a contributing factor to make a move, if you've identified your interest in home building, don't wait too long to get started. When you have your youth, you have the most energy, the most confidence, the least baggage, and, generally, the fewest obligations.

At the end of the day, the point of the story is that the moment you identify your passion for something, don't ignore it. Move as quickly as you can and don't worry so much about timing or the economy, because the real purpose is to do what you love and to start enjoying the rest of your life as soon as possible.

Starting a new business does come with some side effects, especially if you are established in your career and with existing financial obligations. Once you have a family, your reality is different and you have a much bigger dilemma. The choice whether to pursue your dreams and risk not being able to support your family is tougher. Sometimes life gets difficult, and, with a family of my own, I personally tend to be more cautious and responsible than a dreamer, but that is just a personal choice. In cases like this, I recommend prudency to ensure that your loved ones are well taken care of before you jump in. Avoid putting them, not to mention yourself, in a bad situation. To do that, it's necessary to have enough money set aside for any contingencies before you make the leap to entrepreneurship.

Setting up your business officially

Once you make the decision to get into the home building business, there are a number of steps I would recommend you take to improve your chance of success, both in the short- and long-term. Taking time to establish your company and laying the groundwork for business systems will prevent many problems down the line.

The first thing to do is to set up your financial system. This is what I equate to the instrumentation in the cockpit of a plane. You're the pilot of your business, but you're going to need to rely on reporting systems to know how you're doing and where you're headed. Setting up systems for tracking and reporting your income and expenses before you become overwhelmed is smart; don't wait until you have piles and piles of receipts to record. You don't want to have to try to reconstruct those expenses after the fact. That's like deciding where you're headed once you're already up in the air in your plane. You'll waste lots of time and energy putting accounting off until later, believe me.

Setting up your business should be your first priority, and you can start by managing your accounting with a simple software program like QuickBooks, FreshBooks, Wave, or something similar. That will help you categorize your income and expenses as it comes in.

Then find an accountant, preferably a certified public accountant (CPA), who specializes in real estate. Not all accountants are equal or have the same training and experience, and a general accountant is not going to be as useful to you as someone who understands the intricacies of real estate and construction. An accountant who specializes in real estate will understand the guidelines, the regulations, the allowances, deductions, and the laws that impact your business. If you don't find a real estate specialist, you risk getting advice that is not correct for your specific business. That can cost you time and money down the line.

Information is the mother of clarity, vision, and decision-making in business management. Without information about your business' performance, it's impossible to pilot the plane. Which is why you need to be able to reference all of your expenses immediately from the day you start your business. You need to be able to see what you spent, where you spent it, and what deposits you took in. You also need to categorize everything, so that you know what type of expense you had. For example, was the money you spent for a development expense a carrying cost, an administrative cost, soft cost, payroll, for framing, for demo? If you don't want to categorize each up-front, as you make the payment, you will absolutely hate trying to recall what the money was spent on later. It's easy to get confused.

Setting up even simple money management and accounting systems from the start also enables you to track how your money is being spent and to derive statistics about your company's performance. Being able to run statistical analyses of the money coming in and going out will tell you what you're doing right and what's not going as well as you had expected, so that you can make adjustments before it's too late.

Your recordkeeping process or system does not have to be sophisticated, but it does need to make it easy for you to regularly make note of every penny you've earned and spent within the business. Collecting scraps of paper and receipts in a big pile is not useful. You need a way to file those records away so that when viewed all together, they tell the story of how your business is doing. Let's not forget that banks and investors will need them, and the cleaner and clearer they are the more credibility you will have.

In this business, paying close attention to your cash flow, or where your money is, can make the difference between being wealthy and being bankrupt. You can be very wealthy on paper, with several properties worth hundreds of thousands or even millions of dollars, but if you don't have enough cash to pay the mortgage on those properties while you try to sell them, you are effectively broke, and about to get more broke if the bank forecloses on them. If you don't have cash, you will be out of business soon. Which is why it's essential to plan and to understand where every dollar is going.

Cash management is essential to a business, which is why in the balance sheet portion of every set of financial statements, the section related to assets is broken into two: current assets and non-current assets. Although both represent money that you have, they are very different categories. One is immediately accessible, called "liquid," and the other one is inaccessible or non-liquid. One can solve your immediate problems and the other one can't.

Let's imagine that you have ten construction projects "in progress." You invested $100,000 of your own money and the bank lends you an additional $400,000 to build each of them. Essentially, you are a millionaire! But this million is basically inaccessible until you finalize and sell your projects. Meanwhile, if you don't maintain the correct cash reserves to make your interest and other payments, you could lose your million worth of equity overnight when the bank forecloses on the properties. That is how fortunes are lost.

Understand that there is a difference between accounting and finance, too. Finance is about understanding the language of money, making sense of it, and turning your data into information. It's about making the best use of all your resources. This is basically financial engineering, because it has to do with how you utilize your assets and move them around to maximize them. While accounting is the system of tracking each and every dollar, recording and documenting what you do with your money—the exact bookkeeping aspects of entering details regarding the money coming in and going out—finance is the art of interpreting accounting and making the best use of money.

How you plan to grow or to report all the money you've made and spent can be impacted by how you've decided to structure your business. Choosing the type of corporate entity your business will be classified as is another important first step in setting up your home building business.

Making it official

Although you have the option to run your business as a sole proprietorship, which is the simplest form of business entity available, I strongly urge you not to take that route. Sole proprietorships are not advised for real estate ventures. No, I'm not an attorney, so please consult one before you get too far, but for liability reasons alone, a sole proprietorship provides little to no protection for your other assets should someone ever sue you.

Creating a separate entity for your business is smart, as opposed to operating as an individual (a.k.a. a sole proprietorship). Setting up a separate business entity will essentially build a barrier between you, personally, and the business, by providing you with some protection in the event that something goes wrong on one of your properties. For that reason, the most common types of entities to set up are a limited liability corporation (LLC) or a Subchapter S corporation. These formats provide you the best available protection while generating no additional taxes because they are considered pass-through entities, meaning that whatever the business profits, the corresponding taxes are paid by you personally.

> If you don't yet have a small business attorney and want to get your business officially established, one option is to use an online business service that will create your entity for you as part of a package. I've used BizFilings, but there is also The Company Corporation and LegalZoom, as well as many others that can assist in getting all your paperwork squared away and filed for you.

Whatever type of legal entity you choose, I do recommend creating one because chances are that sooner or later something will happen at one of your job sites that you will be blamed for. It is only a matter of time before someone trips and falls inside your property, steps on a nail, or a customer gets upset with how something was completed in their home, regardless of how much you try to prevent it.

To maintain this corporate shield, you need to first select the type of organization you prefer and, second, treat it and operate it as if it is completely separate from your personal finances. Do not commingle expenses or checkbooks, keep business and personal completely separate.

Creating an organized operation

Running a business involves a lot of moving parts, from coordinating subcontractors and schedules to communicating with buyers, responding to attorneys and accountants, and taking care of dozens of other tasks that crop up during a typical day or week. To ensure that you're completing everything that needs to be done, in order of priority or importance, you need to be organized. In fact, I would go so far as to say that the survival of your business depends on your ability to be organized and *stay* organized. And if you surround yourself with employees and contractors who are themselves organized, you will be much better off.

When faced with a choice between an experienced job applicant and a super organized one, I will go with the super organized one every time. You can teach people the business but it's challenging to teach a naturally disorganized person how to become organized. To be sure that you're dealing with someone who is familiar with setting up and using systems in their daily life, ask specific questions during job interviews about what they mean when they claim to be organized. Allow them time to articulate what being organized looks like to them. For example, how do they take notes? How do they file them so they can easily be found again? How do they plan their day? How do they approach prioritizing tasks? How do they juggle routine duties with the unexpected crises or "fires" that crop up and have to be dealt with immediately?

Having job candidates walk you through how they manage their own lives can provide a look into how they would perform on the job. You want someone who plans out their day the night before or even days prior, who balances their checkbook regularly, and who takes notes during important discussions and has a way to file and retrieve them later. Those types of people will only help your business run more smoothly.

As your business grows, keeping track of what's occurring with every task will become essential, and you need people working alongside you who are as concerned about the details as you are. You want to ask, "Where is that survey we ordered on the Smith house?" and hear details in the response, "I ordered it from XYZ on April third, I followed up on such and such date, and yesterday I contacted them to confirm that it is due to us tomorrow." You do not want to hear, "I ordered it," or "They haven't gotten back to me." That's not reassuring.

> There are no bad organizational systems. Find what process works for you and stick with it. The only bad system is one that isn't used.

Being organized is the mother of productivity, efficiency, and success.

Starting a business with limited resources

Most entrepreneurs I've come in contact with started their companies with limited resources, meaning money they had managed to save or borrow from family and friends. Very few had access to unlimited amounts of cash. Unless you've already had success in another venture or career, you're probably in the same boat—trying to figure out how to start your home building company with the least amount of money possible, so as not to disrupt your family's lifestyle.

Even if you have managed to stash away some cash to tide you over while you're building your business, it's probably not enough, or not as much as you could use. The reason I say that is because from the time you file your incorporation papers to the day you sell your first home, it's likely to be more than a year. Even if you go the route of being a flipper, for example, where you do strictly cosmetic work or upgrade only some parts of an existing house, depending on the scope of work, you may be able to turn the project around in three to six months, but that would also require an investment. For this reason, many people start building homes as a part-time business while still fully employed. This is one of the best and most common ways because even though it will put a lot of pressure on your schedules and make for very long workdays, at least you still have an income coming in.

Another good way to start is to become a subcontractor or skilled tradesman to an existing home builder, if you have experience with painting, carpentry, or floor installation, for example. That will give you access to quick cash as soon as you're given a job. This approach is also common and gives you gradual experience in home building without putting pressure on your personal finances.

Of course, if you picked up this book, you probably want to skip all that and start building a house from the ground up, and you can, so let's discuss the options.

Perhaps the best way to reduce your investment outflow is by becoming a custom home builder, because there are several ways to get the necessary capital from your client. The issue is that initially, it might be difficult to get someone to give you a custom job without any experience. Further ahead we'll discuss ways to raise capital with creative financing, as well as the pros and cons of pre-selling homes, but for now, let's first identify the basic concepts of these options.

We can go the "spec home builder" route, meaning speculative, as in unsold, or as a "custom home builder," which means building for a specific client. These are different but what makes these models confusing is that people casually refer to them interchangeably. For example, there are builders that start their project as a "spec," without a buyer and hoping to find one along the way. But they call it a custom home because of its high-end, high-priced, detailed and intricate characteristics designed for wealthy buyers. However, because they do not have a buyer at the outset, it's technically a spec home.

Just the same, some builders may rename a spec home the moment it sells, calling it a custom even if it started as a spec house. Once sold, the house went through some level of upgrades, changes, and special requests, which somewhat customized it. In my opinion, a spec or speculative home, by definition, is one that began without a buyer, and a custom is one that was designed and built for a specific homeowner from the ground up. There are no in-betweens regardless of uniqueness and price point.

That is also the way that a lender will define it. Let me also clarify that there's a distinction between pre-selling or selling a spec home at some stage versus designing and building a custom home. You can certainly pre-sell a home in one of your developments, which is very common, but that doesn't make it a custom home; it simply becomes a "pending home" if it's still under an option period or a "sold home" once the buyer's option period expires. We'll delve into that in future chapters.

Ironically, when you have no previous experience in the industry is when you are most likely to become a speculative builder. The reason is that it may be difficult to find a client to build a custom job for when you have no résumé. This means tightening your belt, raising and gambling equity capital.

When Tristan and I started out, we did not take a single dime of profit for almost five years (true story). In all honesty, I never imagined that it would take that long; I did not plan for it or predict it. As far as I knew, we would make money on our first project and just take off from there. I wish someone had warned me.

Don't ask me how we made it through without an income for so long because that's an entirely separate story for another book. All I can say is that we were so persistent and willing to do whatever it took to make it happen—working crazy hours without focusing on the money, just knowing that failure and defeat were not an option. Then one random day, I am not sure how, the money started pouring in.

We went into it with our eyes closed somewhat, or at least blind to what to expect and when. We had some savings but no sense of whether it would be enough to sustain us. It was an extremely difficult journey, and we lived one day at a time during those first five years. I am not suggesting that it will also take you this long, but that's how it went for us. In retrospect, I am glad that during that time, we never got ahead of ourselves by spending money from any of our projects under the assumption that they would generate a profit. We never spent money we didn't have, and even the money we did eventually earn, we figured out how to restrain ourselves financially and reinvest the majority of it. Constantly reinvesting in the business was a huge component of our ultimate success.

The point is that in this business nothing is assured, and you need to be realistic with your expectations and know what you're getting into. Unfortunately, a common mistake that new builders make is to start without enough of a financial cushion. Too often builders underestimate how long it will take to develop, permit, prepare the land, break ground, build the house, market, and sell it. The process of turning a property is frequently much longer than new builders anticipate.

But the even bigger mistake I've witnessed is overconfidence, or the assumption that you are going to be successful right away. To think that you won't have a learning curve and that you'll hit a home run your first time up at bat is possible but improbable. It's important to have self-confidence, yes, but it also needs to be realistic. It's much smarter to hope for the best and still prepare for the worst. That's the approach we took. That didn't mean that we didn't expect to be successful *eventually*, because we did, but we purposely were conservative in our revenue projections. The truth is, there will be surprises you couldn't have accounted for or expected. Those surprises will increase your expenses and extend your timeline. That means your profit will shrink and the date on which you thought you'd have your money will likely be pushed out into the future. If you expect that and plan for those kinds of surprises by putting money aside, you will be much better positioned for success.

Don't get impatient

The problem with burning through your savings before you hit that home run is that as your personal savings start to dwindle, you'll start to look for ways to pull money out of the business. You'll get creative. Normally, creativity is a virtue, but when you're making decisions driven by an urgent need for money, your choices may not be in your business' long-term interest. Sure, it might get your mortgage paid for this month, but it could also put at risk any money you had expected to make when you sell the property. So be careful about moving money around or taking money out when you hadn't originally budgeted for it to be used that way.

Another potential pitfall has to do with tacking on expenses to each draw you may take as progress payments. Let's say you're building a house but don't yet have a customer, so the bank has agreed to give you access to funds as you complete different parts of construction. Those payments are called "draws." They are partial advances you're taking out of the total budget for the project. So, you'll get a draw when you finish your foundation and your framing, and then your roofing and insulation and drywall. Sometimes builders will tack on fees to those draws to cover their expenses, assuming that once the house is finished and sold, there will be excess money in the form of profit that will more than cover these expenses. That's one way to go about it but it's risky, because depending on the market when you go to sell, you may not earn as much profit as you had anticipated, and you may have to pay back some of the money you took out for your expenses.

You should never use money that has been allocated for the construction and development of the home for any of your overhead. If you need money to cover other expenses then you need to find it somewhere else, such as from reserves, investors, or from your savings, but not from your construction or development budget.

The bank that lent you the money trusts and assumes that you're staying current with all of your bills. After all, if you fall behind, they don't need to be concerned because they have a first lien position. That means they will be repaid first, in full, whenever the property sells, even if you have to take a loss. So, they're not as worried, but you should be.

I would also strongly recommend that you keep funds separated by project. Don't mix revenue and expenses across all the houses you're working on. Instead, set up separate accounting so you can better track all of your expenses and the payments you've made for each property. You need to be able to differentiate and recognize when and why projects are going over budget, so that you can improve with each home you build. That includes not paying from one development to cover an extra expense on a different house; moves like that can really mess up your accounting. Only by maintaining separate records for each house can you get an accurate sense of where your money is being spent, what project is going well or not so well, and when specific costs are going over budget.

Another common tactic I don't recommend early on is the use of management fees as part of your project budgets. Tacking on management fees to cover some of your business' overhead puts added pressure on each project's finances and makes it more difficult to be profitable.

A better approach is to be conservative when estimating profits and liberal when estimating your expenses. That way you build in a cushion if something goes awry early on with a house. And if you end up selling the house for more than you projected, so much the better. But you absolutely don't want to discover too late that you've overspent on construction and won't even make the money you've invested back. That makes it hard to move onto a new project if you don't have any profits to reinvest. If you want to go from one project to two, then you need to start saving some of the money that you made on earlier developments. You want to be able to take profits and reinvest them by buying another plot of land. That's how a business grows organically.

Part of that ability to reinvest proceeds from the sale of a house comes to being frugal generally. Don't overspend, in your business or your personal life. You don't need a fancy office or a fancy car or a bigger house right now. By taking money out of the business and spending it on things that won't directly improve the company, you're making it more difficult to grow. An expensive lifestyle will not help your next house sell for more money.

Unfortunately, I have seen too many builders come and go quickly. They build one project, lose money, and walk away to do something else because they didn't make the windfall they expected. This is not a short-term game, but as long as you're improving with each build, you have the potential for a long and profitable career in home building.

Creating a personal manual of operation

After discussing some of our potential financial limitations, it is fair to say that during your early stages, it's likely that you will be doing most of the work yourself, with very little to no help. That's no easy task. Besides financial mismanagement, another mistake I've seen some business owners make is focusing too much on one area of the business, to the detriment of all others. Maybe they love marketing, so they invest most of their time and energy in finding ways to promote the business, rather than managing the construction process, or vice versa. Or maybe they have a lot of experience in interior design and spend far too much time getting the finishes on a home just right. But neglecting even one area of the business can have a negative impact on operations and on profitability. If you take your eye off cost control, expenses will likely increase and cut into your profits. Or maybe you got so wrapped up in selling a couple of your houses that you stopped looking for new lots to build on, so your business will probably have a lull until you find more properties to buy.

In this business, you're a lot like an air traffic controller. You can't be so focused on just one plane that you don't pay attention to all the others taking off and landing at the same time. You need to regularly take a step back, to view your business from a 30,000-foot view. Only that way can you see what's going well and what's being ignored. From that vantage point, you can shift your focus to correct anything that needs attention.

I tend to do this fairly regularly in my own company. I'll stop to reflect and review where I could be working more efficiently, or where I'm dropping the ball. And in doing this, I'll realize that I don't have new contracts for land, so I need to shop for them. Or maybe I'll see that I've been so focused on building up my inventory that I forgot all about expediting new permits. Or perhaps I've been too focused on the administrative and land development that I haven't made as much progress on the actual construction of houses.

This is a business where you need to constantly be juggling multiple balls. And it's important to keep all of them in the air—you can't let one drop. Every aspect of your business is equally essential to your success.

That said, you get to decide for yourself how you'll manage your time and all the various aspects of your home building business. That's your personal operating manual.

Normally, contractors start at 7:00 a.m. and work Monday through Saturday until the tasks they needed to complete that day are done. That's usually until around 6:00 or 7:00 p.m. And unless you have someone to whom you can hand off the responsibility of unlocking the gate in the morning to let contractors in, you'll need to build that step into your day. Once your day starts, you'll need to be available at the job site to answer questions.

In general, the balls you'll need to juggle each day include your:

- ✦ Administrative duties (creating budgets; reviewing invoices; filling out purchase orders; writing checks; wiring funds and paying bills; opening accounts for your utilities; property taxes; looking through title work; evaluating new opportunities; reading contracts and documents; preparing loan requests; balancing your accounts; posting expenses; creating reports; estimating expenses, and the list goes on)
- ✦ Physical duties (locking and unlocking sites; scheduling your subcontractors; calling repeatedly to confirm their presence; being there to direct and show support; confirming accuracy

of work according to plans; ensuring quality; meeting with inspectors and passing inspections; making decisions on every construction step; correcting changes and errors; monitoring selections and finishes; answering questions; maintaining order and cleanliness; visiting new potential sites; evaluating the competition, to name a few)
- Back of the house (studying every corner of your architectural plans; discussing details with engineers, plan checkers, city officials, attorneys, title companies; filling out water/sewer applications; applying for permits; following up on plan revisions; drafting easements and common area agreements; working with real estate agents; meeting with prospects and buyers; and many more)

Together these categories of activities and the individual tasks you have to complete or review regularly form your manual of operations. That's your list of what you need to be paying attention to and what results you're expecting to see.

Although you may close down your job site at 6:00 p.m. when your subcontractors leave, there may be other tasks you need to attend to after that. Because crews get paid by the job, not the hour, they try to be as efficient as possible. For that reason, you'll want to supervise their efforts to be sure they're also providing the level of quality you expect.

Your subcontractors are essentially acting on your behalf, and you want their workmanship to reflect the type of work you want your company to be known for, whether that's custom, traditional, contemporary, or Mediterranean.

Creating your company's corporate image

It's important to realize that as you're making early decisions about how you want your company to operate, you are effectively creating a corporate image. Building a home, building a name, and building a brand are all connected. Which is why you need to decide early what you want your company to look like a few years down the road. What are your business goals? What type of company do you hope to run in five or ten years? Then you need to create a business image that matches that long-term goal.

To build a brand that reflects where you want to take your company, you need to think through elements such as:

- Your company name
- Your logo
- Marketing materials
- A uniform – T-shirts with your logo for you and your team
- Giveaways, like mugs and pens
- Photography
- How you'll present project proposals and renderings of buildings
- A company website
- Social media accounts
- Signs to place in front of your properties

The attitude you adopt with respect to business, meaning how you interact with prospects and contractors and government officials, will also shape your brand, or how others perceive you and your company. Act organized and corporate from day one and that's the reputation you'll earn.

The steps you take now to set your company up properly, with systems and processes in place to make you as efficient as possible, will make it possible for you to scale your company as quickly as you want. The more you do now, early on, to prep yourself for success, the bigger your rewards will be down the line.

CHAPTER 3

Surround Yourself with the Right Team

Although you may feel like a solo entrepreneur initially as you start your home building business, the good news is that you won't be for long. This company you're forming is a lot like a band. You're the conductor, or the lead singer, and before you can start booking paying gigs, you need to pull together your key bandmates—the people who will help determine your results. So, you need a drummer, a bass player, and other instrumentalists to start. Without them, you can't move forward.

In addition to finding skilled performers, you also need people who can work well with others. You don't need a team of wannabe superstars who will be wrestling for the limelight. You really need people who will be cooperative and who will approach situations like a teammate.

The same is true in the home building business. You need to surround yourself with top performers who have the skills and market knowledge you need to be successful. But before you can start putting together your group, you need to be clear about the type of homes you're building, so that you can recruit talent that knows your market. You may be able to attract a super real estate agent with an impressive track record, but unless he or she knows the neighborhoods you're targeting, they are not your best choice. Being an expert in the town ten miles away is not as useful to you as knowing the ins and outs of what has sold in the five-block radius you want to specialize in.

Now, there are several parts of your business. Just like a band has vocalists and instrumentalists, or like a football team has many positions, you're going to need a construction team that can tackle the different aspects of the business as well as an experienced sales team, each of which has very different skillsets.

Finding a top real estate agent

Your real estate broker or agent is one of the first additions you should make to your team, because they have the knowledge to help you find a property to build on. Brokers or agents are also useful for advising you regarding the current market and what buyers are looking for. Land is your true raw material. You can find the materials required to build a house—lumber, nails, drywall, paint—almost anywhere, but you can't necessarily find affordable, buildable land as easily. That's the toughest part of this business, I think, and if you can master locating suitable land for building, you will have a major advantage.

All that starts with finding your broker (assuming you're not one yourself). So how do you know which brokers are the best? This is a tricky question, believe it or not. In some respects, working with the top volume producer makes sense because they know what works and what doesn't. However, they may also try to steer you too much in whatever direction they are familiar with, rather than where your vision is headed. Understanding the precise amount of input needed from your marketing team and blending their goals with yours is up to you. Top producers have proven their sales abilities and are likely to have strong opinions. Always listen to their advice, but at the end of the day, this is your project, your money, and you are the one assuming the risk, not them.

The best partnership is with an agent who meets your criteria. In my experience, those criteria consist of a person who can provide you with a balance of wisdom, helpful suggestions, and constructive criticism, whom you can learn from and who makes sense to you without overpowering your authority or your vision. Someone you understand and communicate well with. You'll achieve the best results when you have a broker by your side who understands what you want and need.

It's all about who you want to work with and who has the best chemistry with you. The bottom line is that if the market is strong, most agents will be able to sell your house. It will come down to negotiating skills. But if the market is bad, they will all likely struggle to sell it, and this is where it's important to team up with a hustler who can bring you prospects and close the sale. Over the years I've also come across agents who I felt were negotiating more with me, the seller, to reduce the price, than with buyers to make an offer. Don't forget that you are part of the equation to help facilitate a deal, which is how they make money.

The difference between an agent versus a broker mainly comes down to the type of real estate license they hold. To get into the real estate business as an agent, you have to obtain a realtor's license and pass the corresponding tests. After a few years, you can take additional training and become a broker. A realtor must work for a broker, but if a realtor chooses to move on and become a broker, they can list properties independently from other firms and hire agents to work for them. There is more work and more liability as a broker, too. But let me caution against assuming that a broker is better or more experienced because they've passed the broker's exam. Just because someone works under a broker does not automatically mean they are any less qualified or experienced; some top performers actually prefer to remain agents rather than build their own empires.

Another factor to consider is your agent or broker's specialty. Every broker, every agent, over time starts specializing. That's true for almost every business, including yours. As you gain more experience, you start to identify which types of houses or client or area or price point is the best for you. The more specialized, the more you start turning down opportunities that aren't the type of project your business is best at. Maybe because they're too far away, too small, or too big, for example. Your specialty, your niche, is your very well-defined target area or client type.

The same goes for some real estate professionals. Over time, they evolve, too, and start to focus more narrowly on a particular neighborhood, style of home, or client, for example. They become known for selling in a certain zip code or serving a particular demographic, such as first-time home buyers or retirees, for example. They become specialists. You want to find someone whose specialty matches your own, whatever it is.

So, if you're specializing in $300,000 homes in city neighborhoods, you want to find an agent who sells more of those types of homes than anything else. You don't want an agent who is selling mainly $2 million homes in the suburbs. Their clients are not your clients, so they are not in a good position to advise you, for example, on what changes to make to your home to make it more appealing to your target buyer. After all, they're not familiar with your target buyer. They're also not mixing and mingling with your target market regularly, or with other agents who are connected to new prospects for your typical price point.

Finding the best contractors and trade professionals

Just as you want to partner with real estate agents who you work well with, who know your target area and ideal buyer, you'll want to hire other professionals, contractors, and subs who spend most of their time working on projects that are similar to your own. You don't want an architect who is known for designing $5 million properties to build your 1,400-square-foot ranch, for example. Sure, they have the expertise to design the smaller home, but it would be out of the ordinary for them. Instead, you want an architect who knows how to squeeze the most living space possible out of the available square footage. You want someone who has designed similar homes dozens or even hundreds of times before. That's much easier when all you build are homes between 1,200 and 1,600 square feet. They need to know your product as well as you do.

The good news is that once you find an architect, engineer, drywall sub, or other contractor, you can ask for referrals to other professionals who specialize in your type of homes. For example, once you find a good surveyor, they can help you find a good environmental testing firm. Or find an architect you like and they can point you to engineers they prefer to work with. One vendor can lead you to another, who leads you to another, so that over time you can bring together a team of contractors who all know the type of house you build inside and out. I am not suggesting that you should build what others are building. You should still apply creativity, innovation, and have an edge that differentiates your product, but don't overdo it, at least until you learn the business.

Although technology and the internet have revolutionized our ability to research and locate anything that we might need, there is still value in personally connecting with other potential subcontractors. I found that one of our best ways of finding new contractors was actually stopping by other construction sites and asking for business cards. The contractors you decide to work with can also become sources of referral to other services you may need, and before you know it, you'll have built your own team.

Finding land

Most entry-level builders will struggle to find ideal lots. Larger builders have established relationships with developers and real estate agents that put them at the head of the line when it comes to buying properties. They get the first chance, and smaller or newer builders are locked out. If you're not part of their fraternity of builders—the group who trade information and opportunities—they're not going to sell you any of their land. And they're especially not going to sell you a small lot here and a small lot there in their development. It's just not in their best interest.

But you're not alone. I've rarely been able to just buy a handful of lots in a development or community being built by a larger company. There is no incentive for them to sell you a lot or two when they can just as easily sell to large companies that have the financial capacity to buy hundreds at a time. Some developers are also their own builders, so it makes more sense for them to just keep them for their future needs.

Which means you're likely going to need to buy vacant lots and tear-downs in older, already developed neighborhoods. Rather than trying to buy in a new subdivision, focus instead on opportunities where you can tear down a dilapidated building and put up a brand-new house. That's how you can get into the business.

Don't waste time initially trying to muscle in on pre-developed land in new subdivisions. Instead, find existing lots with old residential or commercial structures, where the building has already been torn down, or where there is a structure in disrepair that should be torn down, or where you can buy the house for the land value.

Finding these opportunities often comes down to scouring neighborhoods, like I frequently did. I'd drive around town in the early days of the business, just looking at the houses to see what might be something we could afford to buy and tear down. It was my hobby—hunting for houses at night or in my spare time. Even my wife Adriana, as my passenger, got used to our nightly driving routine after dinner, zigzagging block after block checking out properties for sale for hours.

When you spot a random house that's ready to be torn down, do some digging at the county clerk's office or appraisal district to see who currently owns it. Once you know that, you can make an offer to purchase it. You can do the same with a commercial building, or adjoining lots that you can combine and then subdivide.

> If we can find two or more houses that are for sale next to each other, we'll frequently buy both and combine them. We can tear them all down and subdivide the land into a larger community that's more efficient and easier to manage, versus building scattered homes. We can consolidate our efforts in one location and build as many as the city allows on that plot of land.

Normally, the newer you are to the business, the harder it is to find lots. This isn't necessarily because of your experience, but because early on, the lots don't come to you. Meaning, you don't have an inner circle, or a group of colleagues and partners who are alerting you and constantly feeding your company with opportunities. You have to be the one to seek them out on your own.

Over time, however, that will start to shift and you'll do less and less hunting and more gathering referrals from others. Once you've established a name and a reputation in your area, you'll get people calling or texting you to give you a heads-up about a lot you might be interested in. Eventually, the lots will come to you, and if you build a good name for your company and earn the reputation as a closer, they will come to you faster than you can handle them.

When I was getting started in the building business, rather than spreading myself too thin over a wide area, I used to saturate a neighborhood. I'd limit my focus to a few square blocks and I'd buy up as many properties as I could there. Not only were there economies of scale I could take advantage of, with multiple properties in close proximity, but people in my little pocket would get to know us. They'd see our signs everywhere and all of a sudden, I'd start to get phone calls. I'd hear, "Hey, I have a client who's thinking of selling." Or, "I own a property and I'm ready to sell." That's how lots start coming to you, rather than the other way around, but as with everything else, good things take time.

Some of the ways I'd find potential lots include:

+ **Looking for "For Sale by Owner" signs.** Watch for homemade signs that go up in front yards or in windows that tell you the homeowner wants to sell. Then get in touch with them asap. You'll generally find this by driving through neighborhoods regularly, like I did. You can also scan For Sale by Owner (FSBO) websites to see if something has quietly come on the market in your area.
+ **Identifying dilapidated properties.** As I mentioned, if you see a home that is older and not well-kept, check the county's ownership records and get in touch to tell the current owner you might be interested in buying their property. You can tell them, "Let me know when you're ready to sell." Then you're first in line when they do decide to put it on the market.
+ **Getting to know real estate agents in the area.** This is the most important tactic. Just as you may focus your attention on a small area to start, that's what successful real estate agents do, too. So, when you see a for sale sign go up, call and introduce yourself to the listing agent. Let them know you're looking to buy homes in the area, so they can keep you in mind for future opportunities.
+ **Monitoring commercial real estate sites.** I have found a lot of properties through sites like LoopNet or Crexi, and through commercial brokers who don't list their properties on the residential multiple listing service (MLS). Many commercial properties can be converted to residential developments, or inner-city pockets can be converted from commercial or industrial to gated communities. I'm seeing this happening everywhere, including Boston, Chicago, Philadelphia, Dallas, Fort Worth, and Houston. If you're willing to tear it down and clean it up, many cities are happy to have you.

- **Circling back to overpriced properties after they've sat for a while.** Some sellers are overly optimistic, let's say, when they first list their home at an inflated price. Or maybe they don't think the home's issues are a big deal, while buyers get scared off. Consequently, the home sits. The initial interest in the property wanes the longer it stays on the market without offers, and people start to wonder what's wrong with it. If it hasn't sold in sixty to ninety days, it gets less and less likely that a buyer will come forward. That's the perfect time for a builder like you to go back to the seller to see if they've become flexible or realistic with their price. Time can help people come to terms with reality. So, even if properties fall off other people's radars, don't let them fall off of yours. Once a house has sat for a long time, ask if the seller might consider an offer under their asking price, and then take your best shot. You might be pleasantly surprised by how willing the seller eventually becomes.
- **Properties with delinquent taxes.** Owners falling behind on their property taxes could be a sign of financial stress, which means that they could be willing to sell. Looking through tax records for accounts with those characteristics and contacting them offering to buy is another method.

When you're getting started, some real estate agents may not give you preference. One strategy to get their interest and attention is by committing to giving them the listing on the home once you build it. Offering them the listing means they will get the commission when they sell the property to you, which you're going to tear down, and then a commission when you build and sell the new house. They are much more inclined to want to help you when you make it clear that it is in their best interest to do so.

Agents understand that working alongside the right builder could potentially mean a steady stream of listings, through the homes you're going to build. Agents are always working to grow their business and you should do the same by constantly building your network.

At first, it makes sense to work with one agent because your volume doesn't require more, but if you outgrow your agent, don't limit yourself. Get to know as many as you can. You shouldn't feel bad about creating a network of realtors that you can turn to. You may feel a certain allegiance to one broker or agent, but don't get stuck dealing *only* with them. You'll miss out on opportunities in new markets when the time comes. Cast a wide net when it comes to agents. At one point, I had a couple dozen brokers working for me, bringing me deals. Of course, we were operating in many areas of the city and each one knew that if they brought me a deal first, they were entitled to the listing of the new home to be built. There will eventually come a time when you will have the luxury of being selective with your land purchases, rather than having to take whatever is offered to you.

You'll also encounter builders whose plates get so full, and that for whatever reason they need to offload land they had bought. So, don't be surprised if an agent offers you land that's owned by a fellow builder. It's likely their circumstances have changed and they may now be interested in selling. It happens.

Of course, you should also be doing your own research, regularly scouring sites like MLS, Zillow, Homes, Trulia, Redfin—there are a bunch of them, with new ones coming online regularly. Stay on top of what's showing up on real estate websites, in addition to doing your own reconnoitering, including staying connected to wholesalers.

While you're looking for land to build on, I would caution you against buying more than you can handle at once; I've made that mistake. Don't buy too many at one time. After realizing how difficult it is to find those first few lots, when a good one comes along, even if you don't need it, the natural inclination is to grab the opportunity. If you don't watch yourself, you can quickly get in over your head trying to do too much too soon before you have mastered the process. Don't run before you can walk.

This is also the time to make sure you have your act together financing-wise. We'll talk about this in more detail shortly, but understand that if you have all your financing lined up and are ready to close, you're in a much stronger negotiating position with sellers. And although you might assume a seller's priority is getting as much money as possible for their house, different sellers want or value different things.

One seller might want to sell their property for as much as possible, no matter how long it takes. Another seller could be more concerned with locking down a sale; they want a sure thing more than they want to maximize their profits. Someone else might want to close as soon as possible, maybe due to a deadline to buy another house. Others might want a shorter option period, more earnest money, a bigger option fee, or quicker closing, and if you have all your financing lined up, you have a better chance of making the deal work.

Minimize buying up land with borrowed money for more than your immediate needs. It is much more difficult to unload a piece of land in a bad economy than to unload a house. If you think that selling a house in a bad market is hard, you haven't tried to sell a lot and get close to what you paid for it. It's next to impossible. While you can pretty easily fire-sale a house and still recover your cost, because you have your profit from your work built into it, that isn't the case with land. Also, your pool of buyers is exponentially smaller when selling land. Your buyers are typically developers and if the market turns, they will all be busy putting out the fires in their own business. They probably won't be in a position to take any land off your hands unless it is at cents on the dollar. To avoid this, don't buy more land than you can build on in the short-term.

Earnest money contracts

When you make an offer to purchase a property, you provide a signed contract establishing the terms and conditions of your offer.

This written agreement is delivered to the seller with your deposit. That money is called earnest money and it reflects how serious and committed you are to buying the real estate. By making this deposit, once the contract is executed by both parties, you are effectively claiming the property, taking it off the market and claiming the exclusive right to purchase it.

The form that you use to make the offer can be the standard state-provided real estate document that your realtor will prepare and fill out for you, or you can pay an attorney to prepare your own earnest money contract form. For your first few contracts, there is no need to take this extra step. It is unnecessary until you are handling large volumes. Many builders have their own contract written up for their use by their attorney, but starting out you'll probably want to use the state-issued contract. However, if the seller provides something other than the state contract, it would be a good idea to have an attorney to look it over, because there is likely something in there that is not in the state version and that could come back to hurt you down the road.

I actually got burned not too long ago because I failed to do just that. I made an offer on a commercial property and the seller sent me their own earnest money contract, and because I was so busy with dozens of other deals and a little too self-confident that I had seen it all, I signed it without truly inspecting it carefully.

Long story short, the deal didn't work out, so I terminated the contract. I did it by email before the 5:00 p.m. deadline on such-and-such date and thought it was all taken care of; that's how most contracts are terminated today, by email. Then I received notification that the deal was, in fact, not terminated. I was confused, so I called the seller and was told I should re-read the contract I had signed. Sure enough, right in the middle, in small print, was the requirement that I needed to send notification of termination by certified mail to a specific address within the deadline. And I hadn't done that. So, failing to catch the fine print cost me $50,000.

I have many other similar stories about when I lost money on transactions, but the main message I want you to take away here is that you need to read contracts and documents carefully, and if there is some item that is not fully clear to you, have the other party explain their understanding of it and then make your own conclusions, to cover all your bases.

Although different in every state, most earnest money contracts are fairly self-explanatory. You need the name of the seller, the name of the buyer (which should be the name of your LLC or corporation), the description of the property, its physical and legal address, and an indication if you are going to have a finance contingency (you specify how much you're going to finance and how much you're paying in cash). The rule of thumb for an earnest money deposit is one percent. Which means that if you're buying a $500,000 property, you'll be expected to put $5,000 down as an earnest money deposit.

However, you're also going to ask for an option period, for which you'll pay an option fee. You'll note how many days you want as part of your option period, during which you'll determine if the project is feasible. That option can be anywhere from a handful of days to sixty or ninety days and even longer, depending on the size and complexity of the project.

The option period fee, also called a feasibility period fee, is a much smaller payment than the earnest money deposit—normally .1 percent. On a $500,000 house, your option fee would be $500. What that .1 percent fee represents is the cost to put the house under contract and retaining the option to terminate the deal during that option period. Both amounts get credited back to you at closing if you move forward.

Almost every contract is going to include a feasibility period. So, if you negotiate a thirty-day option period, which costs you $500, and you discover during the thirty days that there is no way to make the financials work on that deal, or you find something you don't like about that particular property, you can terminate it and you'll only lose that option fee—$500 in this example, rather than your earnest money deposit of $5,000.

SURROUND YOURSELF WITH THE RIGHT TEAM

However, once the option period expires, your earnest money is also at risk if you don't close.

You'll also want a financing contingency, so that if you don't get your financing approved within the specified window of time, you can terminate and still get your earnest money back.

Other options you'll want in the contract include:

- The option to transfer the contract or assign it to another entity
- Selecting the title company and specifying who pays for the title policy
- Specifying the number of days to order a survey
- Indicating the number of days to object to any title or survey issues
- Special provisions
- Attorney approval

Something to be aware of is whether the property is currently occupied and

---

The special provisions section of the contract is usually left blank for you to add notes regarding any specific requests or concerns you have. For example, I usually add that the contract is contingent on the property having dimensions of X feet by X feet, or being no less than X square feet. This is important if you have preliminary plans for your project that will only work given certain measurements. If you're assuming the lot marketed as 5,000 square feet is 50 feet by 100 feet and it turns out to be 46 feet by 109 feet instead, that can destroy your plans.

I also add under special provisions that the seller will either provide utility service accounts or terminate all of the accounts by closing them on or before the closing date. This ensures you don't have any problems closing them later or dealing with a balance on the account. You can also stipulate that the current owner will cooperate with any signatures needed for the purpose of your due diligence, to avoid any problems getting requests with the city filled.

If you have any concerns that don't fit in other sections of the contract, add them in the special provisions area.

---

whether the occupant is the owner or a tenant. If it's a tenant and they have a long-term lease, you may get stuck with that tenant for a long time. So, make sure you get a copy of the lease, if there is one, and that in the contract it states that possession of the property occurs the day of closing. In some states, tenants must be out by then, but in others, the lease could be upheld, so check your state's tenancy laws to be sure you're clear about what could happen if the tenant does not vacate the premises on the day of closing. The best situation for you as the buyer is that there is a month-to-month lease, because that type of lease can generally be terminated at the end of the current month with notification in most states.

But dealing with tenants is a challenge that is best left to the seller as much as possible.

Aside from the earnest money contract, another issue you'll want to pay close attention to is the property's title.

The importance of title work

When you place a property under contract, you work through a title company, which is in charge of processing the entire transaction according to your state's regulations. They are the intermediary responsible for ensuring the proper transfer of title, which is the ownership of the property.

The first step in the process of buying a property, once the contract is executed, is opening title, followed by requesting a title commitment. This is called "opening escrow."

In plain English, a title commitment is a proposal from the title company to sell you an insurance policy under certain conditions. The title commitment begins with the company doing what's called a title search, which involves investigating the chain of title or ownership history of the property. Once completed, the title company presents you with a title commitment. However, this does not mean that everything has gone as expected and that you're cleared to close.

There are four basic sections of the title commitment: Schedule A, Schedule B, Schedule C, and Schedule D. Schedule A is a description of the policy they are offering together with all the basic facts that the transaction represents. Schedule B, in my opinion, is what everyone needs to pay the most attention to, because this is where you find any exemptions and exclusions from coverage. That is, what the title company will not guarantee or will not cover any losses against.

Schedule B lists any restrictive covenants the property has that the company uncovered that apply to the property and for which they won't be held responsible. They're effectively telling you that if you buy the property assuming you can use it in such a way and later find out it's not possible, you can't hold them accountable because the company is disclosing it under the coverage exceptions. For example, let's say you bought a commercial building and planned to tear it down and build apartments but later find out there is an industrial restriction or setback that interferes with your plans, or that the property has to have a specific use. These can all scuttle your plans, but you can't blame the title company.

More commonly, you might discover that your plans are for a gated community but the restrictive covenants expressly prohibit a gate. Or maybe there is a restriction on fences over a certain height.

The problem here is that the title commitment doesn't always give you a copy of the original document listed in this exhibit describing the restrictions—only the volume and page where you'll find the reference. To determine if those restrictions are material to my project, I read through Schedule B carefully and look for any document that was recorded that represents an exemption and I request a copy of the document from the title company—you should too. They could represent easements or you could be granting a common area you hadn't planned on, for example. Until you read them, you really don't know what is in those documents.

Typically, you don't need to worry as much if you're buying an existing home to renovate, but when you're buying a home to tear down and replat it, it matters a lot. When you apply for your permits, the city planning department is going to go through your title documents with a fine-tooth comb and if there are any restrictive covenants that contradict your plans, you will have your project rejected.

Schedule C is also important but not as critical for you to examine as B. This section describes everything that the title company will require to receive, fix, clear, and clean up before the closing in order to provide that policy. These are the problems the company has identified that they will fix with the assistance of the seller. For example, maybe there are two sellers but only one signed the contract, or there are existing liens that must be paid prior to closing, or perhaps there are probate issues to resolve, just to name a few situations. The title company will resolve everything listed, but if they can't, it could delay the transaction.

Schedule D is another section describing more details about the title company, its fees, who the underwriter is, the breakdown of premiums, arbitration requirements, and others.

Once you close and all the documents are executed by both parties, you will receive the title policy itself from the underwriter a few days later.

There are three common types of title policies: a buyer's policy, a lender's policy, and an ALTA policy. The buyer's policy protects you against any title issues and liens, such as if Cousin Freddie shows up three months later claiming ownership, the title company will protect you as the new owner. The lender's policy protects the bank or mortgage company. And there's also an extended policy, called ALTA after the American Land Title Association, which covers the buyer against a longer list of things and which some banks require.

There is also a type of policy called a binder, which is used by investors, builders, flippers, and construction loans, which is a much less expensive policy and which provides the option to purchase a title policy in the event that something shows up within up to two years of the closing.

Be aware that your title policy only covers up to the amount of coverage you've bought, rather than for anything else that you may have spent money on. For example, let's say you bought a $300,000 house and someone files a lawsuit claiming ownership that you now have to defend. Even if you've already invested $100,000 on architect fees, engineers, demolition, and property taxes by this point, since your original policy is only for $300,000, that is the maximum you can receive if you lose—not the total amount you've spent.

You might think problems are a rare occurrence, but I've encountered them multiple times through the years. One time, for example, I bought a property from a developer and later someone put a lien on the property before I broke ground. It turned out that the developer had a side agreement with an investor that had never been recorded, so the title company wouldn't have uncovered it. The property got stuck in litigation and the title company ended up having to release the property back to the owner. That cost me a year plus everything that I spent on the project, and I didn't end up with the property.

In another case not too long ago, we bought a decent-sized property from an entity that didn't actually own it. When the owner discovered it, somehow, they sued us and sued the title company to get it back. We hadn't broken ground yet, but we had spent money on the development, which we then lost. I have many examples like this.

These types of situations don't happen very often at all, but when they do, they are extremely disruptive to your business.

Regulatory departments to get to know

There are a number of private and government departments that you'll need to communicate and interact with during the process of permitting, developing, and building. You'll want to get to know them. It's also important to know that they are separate and distinct, rather than part of an umbrella organization or process. Sometimes one hand does not know what the other is doing, is what I'm trying to convey. So, although one department may have no issue with your planned development, it doesn't mean that you won't run into other jurisdictional issues within other departments.

Let me give you an example. Let's say I go to the city's engineering department to get feedback about my proposed project. I tell the engineer, "I want to build this number of homes with these characteristics" and I'm told that it meets all the department's criteria, so I'm fine. But what I may not be told is that I also need to check with the water and sewer department about the new connections, or that the city planning department needs to verify my planned access, plus their own laundry list of requirements. Sometimes departments will contradict each other; one department may agree on something and then later it will be rejected by another because each entity has different purposes.

The good news is that your architect and your engineering firm will get you through everything. If you make the right selection, these two firms will know what to do, whom to talk to, and whom to run your project by to ensure that it's fine. You still need to know all of this—they do make mistakes sometimes—so that you can stay on top of where things stand in the process and what needs to be done next.

Although every city is different, in general, these are the departments you'll want to interact with, in this general order:

- City office
- City engineer
- Water and sewer
- City planning department, which enforces codes
- Local utility, electrical, and cable provider, regarding where lines can run
- Forestry or parks and recreation department, regarding trees and vegetation
- Traffic
- Stormwater pollution prevention

- Historic district if the area is impacted by any historic regulations
- Appraisal district, regarding taxes on the property

Generally speaking, the larger the city or town, the longer the process may take, because representatives have more people to report to, more departments, more complex infrastructures to comply with, and their workload can get overwhelming. However, smaller towns may have fewer demands and fewer individualized departments to coordinate and communicate with, so fewer people making decisions. Also, it is important to point out that some cities have zoning restrictions that make this process different. There are cities historically more business- and development-friendly than others. Some welcome and encourage growth and construction while others resist it. You may want to look at the appetite your community has to incorporate new housing and under what conditions.

Once you break ground and start construction, there are additional departments that will want some oversight, including:

- The Environmental Protection Agency (EPA)
- Occupational Safety and Health Administration (OSHA)

These agencies exist to protect the well-being of the contractors who are working on your project. There are rules and regulations regarding how to keep a safe construction environment that you'll want to become familiar with, to avoid any work stoppage.

As you can see, there are numerous businesses and agencies you'll need to interact with during the course of running your new home building business, and if you put together a strong team, they will keep you out of trouble and ensure steady progress.

CHAPTER 4

Your First Property or Real Estate Deal

Once you've zeroed in on a location where you want to build, found a clear lot or an existing property you can demolish and build on top of, and have that land under contract, it's time to start your due diligence process. Sometimes I'll start this process before the contract is even signed if I'm fairly certain the deal is going to happen, but not if there's some question about it. In that case, I don't want to waste my time and money. Your due diligence involves investigating and uncovering potential obstacles to your plans for the property. Just because the owner assured you that there would be no problem with the title, or that you will be able to split the land into multiple units, does not mean they know what they're talking about.

You now want to turn to reputable sources of information to get all of your questions answered before you proceed to pay for the property you now have under contract. That contract gives you the *option* to buy it, but you are not yet fully committed. At the moment, you are not locked in to paying tens of thousands, hundreds of thousands, or even millions of dollars for it, yet. So, you want to use this option period wisely, to confirm that the information you have about it is correct and that your plans for how you'll use it will be approved. You do not want to proceed to pay big money for the lot and then learn that it's zoned commercial, not residential, or that there's an underground tank that first has to be removed, or that it will cost way too much to bring the water and sewer lines to the property. Which is why you're conducting your own due diligence—your information-gathering process—before you sign on the dotted line.

Performing your due diligence

Let's discuss a few of the basic and fundamental steps that need to be performed in order to evaluate any given property before buying it. This examination is referred to as "due diligence," which is a technical or legal term used to exercise a reasonable amount of investigation that will help you determine if a property is viable, feasible and suitable to be developed in the way that you intend to build on it. This process begins immediately during the option period or feasibility period of the earnest money contract that I previously mentioned. I want to walk you through the basic issues you need to explore.

First, you want to wait for a title commitment. The title, as we just mentioned, is going to provide a lot of background information on the property, such as the name of the current owner—which should match the seller's name—and any outstanding liens on the property. If a person or business has placed a lien on the property, perhaps due to home improvements that were never paid for in full, or there is an existing mortgage, that will need to be cleared before you buy it. Check the title carefully.

Second, get a survey. Request a recent one from the seller and if they don't have one to give you, order your own from a local surveyor. The survey will confirm the legal descriptions, subdivision's information, lot dimensions, square footage, fences, location of any existing structures, driveways, perimeter, any encroachments from this property or the neighbors, recorded easements—ground or aerial—poles, whether you're in a flood zone, the street's right of way (ROW)—meaning how wide the street is—and much more. There are often cases where obstructions will show up, and you want to find out about them sooner rather than later. As long as you pay careful attention, the survey will reveal these things. There may be things you don't want to miss, like a huge tree right where you plan to put a driveway, a fire hydrant where you want to put an entrance, or a neighbor's fence sitting inside of your future property.

When reviewing your survey, look closely at the setbacks and easements, so that you understand what you can and can't fit within the property. You may need to order a topographic survey if the land is not flat or if it sits in a flood zone. Title companies are busy, and it may take a few weeks to get back to you, which is why it's so important to have an option period in your sales contract—to have the time to fully investigate the property.

As part of your due diligence, you want to find out if there is a homeowner association (HOA). If there is one, find out if there is an architectural committee. The more dilapidated or run down the neighborhood is, the less likely there is an HOA, or at least an active one. However, the newer the neighborhood, the better your odds, which means you'll need to request approval for your design before you build. It's the HOA's responsibility to maintain the look of the area, to help its owners maintain their property value. Which means that if you're building in a neighborhood consisting of super modern homes, you will probably not receive permission to put up a Victorian-looking house, or a Tudor. It just wouldn't fit in, and that's what the HOA is most concerned with.

Not only does an HOA maintain the overall look of the homes in the neighborhood, but it is also responsible for supervising the upkeep of all the properties. That can certainly limit your creativity on the home design, exterior appearance, fences and landscaping, as well as adding a cost you'll have to pass along to your buyer for ongoing participation. Homes built within a community that has an HOA pay a fee, which can be monthly or yearly, for those maintenance services. It's a cost over and above their mortgage, which can sometimes put pressure on your asking price. Just be aware of the impact of an HOA at this point, as you're starting to look at properties.

Next, I would start working on a site plan, so you can begin to envision where, exactly, the home or homes are going to be built, so you can confirm that they can be placed where you want them to go. You don't want to encounter any physical obstacles later in the process.

You'll want to visit the city engineer's office, the water department, electrical and cable providers in your area, the civil engineering office, historic office, and city planning offices, which are all listed on your checklist, to be sure that they have no issues with the home you plan to build on that particular lot.

Then you'll want to look at the underground map for your lot. Every city has a map indicating what's beneath the surface, such as where water and sewer lines are. That will tell you how to tap into them or if the existing size allows for new projects. Along with this, you'll want an availability letter from your city water department, which will tell you whether there is enough capacity for the number of homes you want to build. Just because there is water and sewer available does not mean there is enough capacity for your plans. Verify first.

If the property has not always been residential, meaning it was formerly commercial or industrial, for example, you'll want to order an asbestos survey. This is important if you'll need a demolition permit, which is required if you're tearing down anything other than an existing home, such as a warehouse, strip mall, or factory, for example. To get a demo permit, you'll need to present a clean asbestos report.

There is a difference between a Phase 1 environmental Site Assessment and a Phase 2. A Phase 1 ESA is like going to the doctor for your annual physical. It's routine but it will find any anomalies you may want to check out. As part of that Phase 1, you'll get a physical inspection and general history of the site and structure, research of the immediate surrounding area, they'll check for any reported leaks or registered underground storage tanks, and go back through the ownership records for anything unusual. As part of the process a visual inspection will be conducted. If, under the conclusions and recommendations in the report, you're told, "We do not recommend further investigation," you're all set. However, if something unusual is found, either toxins or an unknown drum, for example, the firm will recommend a Phase 2. This is simply a further examination, just like your doctor might recommend you go to a specialist for further investigation of that rash on your hand or the cough that won't go away. You don't have to plan for a Phase 2, but you will want to get an extension to your option period in case you're told the property needs more exploration, and that's if once you receive this information, you still decide to continue investing time on this specific site.

If the property is or has ever been anything other than a single-family residential structure, you'll also want to order Phase 1 Environmental Site Assessment (ESA) from a local environmental company, which is typically the same company that can produce an asbestos report, and if not, they can always recommend one. As part of that, you'll want to request soil samples, where they will have borings done. Boring means they will drill down to ensure there's no contaminated soil, toxic materials, or anything scary hidden below the surface. These tests are not to be confused with the soil samples needed for the purpose of designing your foundation and frame, which we'll discuss later on.

Over the years, we have bought properties that look perfectly fine on the surface, only to find out that there's something buried that shouldn't be there. One time while conducting this research, after drilling under the proposed foundation, we discovered that once you reached eight feet deep, there was trash. Turns out, the location had been a clandestine dumping ground at some point and it was just full of garbage. We still went through with this deal, but the research allowed us to make this discovery, price out the remediation, and renegotiate with the seller to cover that additional cost. We've had other examples, like the time we found some underground tanks that had not been registered with the government and they were not cheap to remove. These things happen!

Another factor to consider is the drainage of the lot. You'll want to explore which way water will drain on your lot, so that you don't create problems for yourself or for your neighbors. That can happen if you put a house at a different elevation than the rest of the neighbors, making it more likely to have water seep into someone's foundation. The city will make recommendations on whether or not the area and elevation require a more sophisticated drainage system design. This is according to different factors, such as your proximity to surrounding neighbors, the particular city's requirements, region, elevations, soil conditions, lot size, and density of your development.

If you plan to replat the property, meaning to change the configuration of the existing lot dimensions to accommodate more homes, you need to talk to your city planning department and all of the other departments connected with municipal services I just mentioned, such as water, sewer, etc. Because if you're converting a property that had two homes on it to, say, eight homes, you need to confirm the multiple guidelines such as minimum lot size requirements and proper access for the additional units.

You'll also want to ask your city what percentage of impervious lot coverage is required. Impervious is the amount or percentage of your lot that will be unaffected by your construction, meaning that it will remain green. For example, you may be told your 3,000-square-foot lot needs thirty-five percent impervious coverage, which means that your building and its amenities can only take up sixty-five percent of that lot. Within that sixty-five percent, you must put your structure, your driveway, your walkway, and anything else connected to the house. The purpose of that impervious set-aside is to ensure the remaining soil has the capacity to absorb water from rain and snow, to properly drain.

Preparing a preliminary budget

While you have the property under contract, meaning that you have the option to buy it if you so choose, you should use some of the time to run some numbers. You need to determine if your plan makes sense and that it will be profitable given what you know so far about the property. That means pulling together a very rough budget, without a lot of detail or specifics, to see if there is a world in which you can make money on this deal.

You won't have time to gather quotes from contractors or to estimate in great detail how much different elements will cost, so you'll need to stick to rough numbers. But even rough numbers will start to shed some light on whether there is profit potential here. Let's call it a Phase 1 of your budget, just to see if it makes sense to proceed. It's not going to be perfect, and it probably won't be 100 percent accurate, but it will give you a very rough idea of whether you can profit on this particular deal, given the current market.

Now, you may wonder why you didn't go through this step *before* putting an offer in on the property, and my answer is that you certainly can. However, if you take too much time to gather this information before you have any right to the property, you will likely miss out and another bidder will come in who already has their act together or that is willing to risk a little option fee money or even full earnest money to get first shot at it. So, yes, you can try to pull together a rough budget before making an offer, but depending on your market, that may not be the best decision. In most cases, it's better to put the offer in, with an earnest money deposit, and include an option period during which you can then run all the numbers to confirm the property makes sense for you. Eventually, once you've

YOUR FIRST PROPERTY OR REAL ESTATE DEAL

done this a few times, you'll get better at estimating these deals in your mind, without putting much time and effort into it.

One of the tricks to creating a preliminary budget that helps you make the right decision is to work backwards, meaning that you first determine what the house can comfortably sell for and only then compile numbers to see if it's achievable. Not many builders do this. Most inexperienced builders gather their numbers first, add them up, and then decide how much they'll need to sell their house for. But since the market will ultimately tell you what your house is worth, rather than the other way around, I wouldn't go that route.

First, start by studying what homes nearby are selling for (request a list of comparable sales from your agent, which are also known as *comps*). Look at your property and then look at those comparable sales nearby to get a conservative estimate of what you could sell the house for. What is the range of prices that houses are selling for here? Don't start collecting quotes and proposals until after you've looked at what homes are currently selling for in your neighborhood, as well as what level of amenities and type of features they offer for that price, so you can confirm that there is a profit margin to be had.

For example, let's say you have the property under contract for $200,000 at land value and you see that new homes of approximately 3,000 square feet on the street behind you are selling for $975,000 to $995,000. Your initial numbers indicate that you can build for around $175 per foot and, after adding land cost, construction, plus all of your other development and soft costs, you're at $860,000, including sales commissions and closing expenses. These figures suggest that according to your rough estimates, you can make some money. Conversely, if you have the property under contract for $200,000 and the market is plummeting and you see those same new homes priced at $875,000 sitting unsold, you may want to take a step back and reconsider your next move.

Try to be conservative as you're running these numbers, to stay out of trouble later on. Rather than taking the highest price any home has sold for in the area, for example, take a price in the middle.

Because even on the same block, there is price variation. There are homes that are on larger lots, some have better views, some sit farther back from the street or have huge, gorgeous trees in the front yard—so there are factors beyond your control that affect why some houses may be more appealing and end up selling for more than others. All of your surroundings should be taken into account as you're determining the right price for your property.

Once you know what homes are selling for in the neighborhood, or what the upside potential is, your next question is what does the house need to contain in order to potentially sell for $975,000 or more? What do other homes at that price point contain, in terms of number of bedrooms, number of bathrooms, and size of backyard, to start? Then look at other features, like whether it has a pool, an elevator, a formal dining room, an eat-in kitchen, or high-end finishes. Does it need a brick façade? How large of a garage? What square footage do we need? What brand appliances, hardware, lighting, and flooring? With that general level of detail, you start working through the numbers.

In that preliminary budget, I then estimate costs within big categories. I don't get very detailed because there are just too many unknowns. But many contractors will give you a ballpark price-per-square-foot. Remember that every city varies and has a completely different cost structure, so what may cost you an average of $150 to $200/square foot in one place could be $275 to $350 in another, or even much more, so you'll want to ask around.

As we just mentioned, to the rough cost to build the house (of, say, $150 to $200/square foot) you'll have to add your land cost, in addition to a list of other expenses. I'm sharing with you a checklist to be used only as a general guide, and which includes items such as land prep, soft costs like architect fees, structural engineer, civil engineer, permits, impact fees, prorated property taxes, the cost to borrow money, and the carrying costs while you own it, so on and so forth. You'll also want to factor in the six percent commission your broker is going to charge you to sell it when it's done, plus the title policy that you will need to buy on behalf of your buyer.

Now, keep in mind that this exercise gets more interesting and elaborate when you plan to build multiple homes on the same lot, but essentially the logic and the math is pretty similar. You will have to play with the options on whether or not it makes better financial sense to build one home according to the comps in the area or to split it and build a greater number of them on the property if the profit looks more attractive assuming that it's allowed. There are cases where the potential of building one larger home on a lot can yield a better return and could have more appeal on a certain block than to build two smaller ones. You need to be the judge of that.

Some builders believe they have such strong negotiating skills that they will be able to cut corners in other parts of the project, such as by getting their contractors to build for $125/square foot instead of $150. If they are successful at beating the contractors up enough to get the price down, what happens is that the contractors then cut corners and may do shoddy work. Or the contractors who are willing to take a lower price may have less experience than you really need or might end up taking much longer to complete the work.

> What many builders do when they neglect to properly evaluate projections is to force the deal by increasing what they plan to sell the house for. If they can't make the numbers work assuming a $650,000 selling price, for example, well, they'll plan to increase the sales price to $800,000 to make the numbers work. Only they don't control the market. Wanting a house to sell for $800,000 does not mean there is a good chance that it will. If you're in a neighborhood where the average home sells for $500,000, it's very unlikely you'll be able to sell a similar home for an extra $300,000 just because you want to; even if you invest more in it, the market doesn't care. I've seen many builders attempt to do so and although everything is possible, it is highly improbable.

Insisting on cost reductions typically means you will see some side effects, including a reduction in quality.

But the point of this whole exercise is to start plugging in some basic numbers to get a sense of the feasibility of the project. Before you officially buy the property you have under contract, get more comfortable with the money you'll need to spend to make the house a reality and to confirm that there is a profit margin when all is said and done.

What you absolutely don't want to do is to buy the property without at least running some of these figures. Do not assume that, no matter what, you'll be able to make the numbers work. You may tell yourself that you can build a smaller house, cut back on fancy finishes or something else to cut costs, but the reality is you simply may not be able to. So, the numbers have to make sense at the outset at least.

Architecture and engineering

Some of the most important players in this process of building a home are your civil engineer, structural engineer, and your architect. Each has their own role to play. Your civil engineering firm is the company that will help you plan and design your project's infrastructure, meaning the site on which you intend to build. The civil engineer will create a plan for the roads, the utilities, and the municipal services that the houses you are building will need. This includes density, gates, proper access, parking, setbacks, green areas, visibility, a utility plan for connecting the water and sewer lines, the storm drains, the electrical, gas, and cable lines, as well as a drainage plan and others. The larger the community, the more complex the civil plans will get.

Civil engineering is less critical, but still necessary to some extent, if you're only building a single-family home on a single lot that's facing an already developed street. However, civil engineering becomes more essential as you build on larger, undeveloped lots (raw land) without any existing infrastructure. The larger the community, the more things to consider.

While we're on the topic of civil engineering, if you have intentions of putting more homes than what is already there on the property you're buying, turning one lot into multiple smaller lots, I should bring up an incredibly important step that needs to be put in motion as early in the game as possible, which is your *re-plat*. I've touched on this during our investigations section, which means the process, approval, and recordation of the new addresses and legal descriptions of your proposed development. This process is not to be confused with your civil permit, which is a completely separate item with different steps and approvals, but your civil engineer will also be able to guide you through both of these. In fact, you will not be able to finalize your civil permit unless you have a recorded re-plat, which is why I tell you to start this step as early as possible. This entire approval is under the jurisdiction of your city planning department.

Managing the water that flows through the property is part of the civil engineer's responsibilities, which generally include plans for water detention and retention. A detention requirement relates to slowing down the water that is being released onto the street from your property. If it rains too much, you need to have a plan to avoid overflowing the street drains. Having a large enough green area that can absorb some of the water helps detain the water from flowing into right of ways, rivers, and public drains.

Retention involves containing and holding the excess water flowing off the property. Every city has requirements for retention ponds based on square feet of land and homes built. Retention ponds capture overflow and hold it so as to avoid overwhelming the public drainage system. Civil engineers make plans to handle the water on and around your property.

Your structural engineer, who is usually selected and hired by your architect, is the person who will help you design the structural components required for your home to be properly supported—meaning to physically maintain the weight of the structure and maintain the integrity of the building. This takes into account your foundation plans, your roofing, framing, the walls, the fasteners, trusses, and the beams, including at what distance they are placed relative to the size of the home.

Before you hire an architect to design a house, it's important to check the land on which the house is going to be built, to confirm it can support a structure. That involves testing the soil and drilling down to check the suitability of the dirt underground to support the building. This is different than the soil samples that were gathered for environmental purposes. These surface and underground investigations are undertaken by a geotechnical engineer. They test for moisture content, density, and type of soil, as opposed to environmentally related issues. These new soil samples will help you ensure it can tolerate the weight of the home you're going to build, without risk of excess shifting

---

Always question your architect and structural engineer. They are the experts but, in some cases, they will overengineer your house in order to protect you and themselves—I'm sure you've heard of CYA (cover your ass). They will overengineer the building because it's easier and safer for everyone. Unfortunately, sometimes this comes with a higher price tag for you. They may put in extra beams or trusses that aren't absolutely needed but that will add to your budget. So, question what they're doing. Ask them to explain why a wall is in a particular position, or if you could save money by having your laundry room back up to a bathroom, or if a less expensive material alternative is possible.

The more experience you have, the more questions you'll be able to ask about why things are being placed the way they are. But even on your first house, ask lots of questions so you can learn why things are done certain ways. Also, your framer can be the best source for a second opinion. Those guys have plenty of experience and can help you identify possible savings without compromising structural integrity.

---

and causing damage. The results will indicate and assist the structural engineer with the correct design of the house according to the properties of the soil, once they know its strength and elasticity (or how much it swells with rain and shrinks in dry conditions), which can impact the foundation.

After you have your plans drawn up, and as you're getting close to breaking ground, depending on your type of foundation, you'll need a building site pad. The pad is an area consisting of very dense soil, also known as loam or select fill, on which your building foundation is going to be placed. It helps prevent your house from shifting. Once the pad is down and has been properly compacted, to really solidify it, you'll run a compaction test to confirm it has been tamped down. Then you should be ready to turn the work over to the construction team. If you go the route of a pier-and-beam foundation, which is raised and has crawl spaces, you will utilize other methods recommended by your engineer to reduce moisture levels, preventing water and humidity from sitting under the home that can cause damage.

Your architect starts with a conceptual design for the house (the vision), which is effectively a big picture of what you want the house to look like and contain. Next, you move to schematics, where the architect lays out the exterior view and appearance, the floor plan for each level, the dimensions of the rooms, and the general traffic flow on each floor. Once you have a draft set of schematics, you'll then start making changes with your architect's guidance. You may want to add a bar area, maybe flip the orientation of a room, add a mud room, make a room downstairs into a mother-in-law suite, or something else that your architect then redraws. After several back-and-forths, you'll finalize your plan and your architect will produce a full set of plans and construction documents, including a final site plan, structural plan, and the mechanical, electrical, and plumbing (MEP) plan to be used to guide the construction process.

All of those plans then need to be presented to your city's construction department for review and approval. This will take some time, so you'll want to keep checking the status online (most departments accept paperwork online these days) to find out when you have the go-ahead, or if there are issues that will need to be addressed first. When initially submitted, you'll be given a registration number or project number to use for following up, future correspondence, and questions.

More likely, the city will have questions or revision requests for you to address, which you'll then hand back to your architect or structural engineer for solutions.

> Structure your payments to your contractors, including your architect and engineers, based on phases of completion. Do not pay them all up-front. Pay them a deposit to get started, then when the plans are completed you pay them another percentage, then when everything is submitted to the city they get another payment, and when the city approves them they get the balance. That way they are always incentivized to help you make it to the next phase.

Building permits 101

You are ultimately responsible for everything your company builds and for ensuring that all requirements have been met, from building permits to codes to municipal regulations. If anything goes wrong, you're the person who will get the phone call or get stuck with the bill. So, you want to be sure your team has followed all of the rules and regulations of your city or county. That includes applying for and receiving all appropriate building permits. Please avoid the excitement of getting ahead of yourself by attempting to break ground prior to having those stamped permits in your hands. Failing to wait for all needed permits will cause you some fines and a red tag an inspector leaves will only delay things further.

Typically, the civil engineer, architect, or plan runner will file all of the necessary permits for you, they will upload and deliver them in person or use a plan runner service so that you don't have to do that work. However, you *do* need to become a micromanager when it comes to permits. Even when you've been assured that all the paperwork has been filed, ask for a copy and project numbers, and always confirm with your own eyes. When you're told that you're just waiting for a response, ask for a date by which you should hear something, and then follow-up with whoever is handling that on your team. Make sure they are actually doing what they are telling you they have done. There's often more than one person working on any given file, with a possible margin for error.

I say this after years of experience with permits and procedures, having been told many times that a project was properly filed and moving along fine: "We're just waiting for an answer" or "It's in the works," only to find out later that the firm hired to do this work got too busy to stay on top of things, or that the person originally in charge of our project was no longer with the company and no one had yet been reassigned to our account. Things do fall through the cracks. Many times no one catches a mistake and, as a result, files unnecessarily sit at someone's desk waiting for an answer, while we assume that things are just moving along as they should. Which is why I'm letting you know that you'll want to stay on top of where your paperwork stands in order to avoid costly delays.

There are permits required for nearly everything, but let's start with the most common and basic ones:

- Demolition
- Re-plat
- Civil or site development
- Construction

As I have mentioned earlier, if you're building a new development "community," you'll need approvals to proceed from several departments, including planning, storm, drainage, structural, traffic, and utilities.

The size of your city dictates how much follow-up and personal contact you'll need to have with each department as well as the level of automation.

Each city has ordinances, which are designed to establish rules regarding how things will operate and grow. Ordinances are created to try to ensure the proper functioning of the city. They are forms of protection, to plan for growth within the area, while also remaining accessible, livable, and enjoyable for residents, by preventing poor planning. What you intend to add to the community needs to exist in harmony with what is already in existence. For example, an ordinance might prevent structures from being built over a certain height or number of floors, so as not to block the view of existing houses or create excessive traffic and chaos.

Codes are local rules regarding how homes need to be built, for the safety of both the homeowner and neighbors. For example, there are building codes regarding what kind of fire alarm must be installed, at what point sprinkler systems are needed, the type of electrical systems acceptable, the rooms that require an operating evacuation emergency window, when a gate for a swimming pool is required, and even the maximum depth allowed for the pool. They are more for safety.

Processes, guidelines, and procedures

When you're just starting out, you're unlikely to have many forms and checklists to work from. As the number of homes you build climbs, the more you will naturally create documents to manage your business. You'll develop standard operating procedures, and also guidelines for the way you want certain processes handled within your business. It is true that in construction it's completely normal for an array of random things to go wrong. It should almost be expected. In our case, as my brother and I began the journey of growing our business, we were honest enough to admit our limited experience in this field. We understood up-front that there would be a learning curve full of surprises, with numerous twists and turns in every step along the way. We also agreed with the fact that problems can often be minimized or even prevented if you learn from them. It was clear to us that making mistakes was acceptable, but what was not acceptable was to continue making the same mistakes over and over. With that philosophy in mind, we made it a point to constantly stop to examine when something went wrong, then learn how and why it happened, evaluate it, come up with a preventive plan, and finally add it to our guidelines, procedures, and manuals of operations. We created these for every department within the business, which we constantly updated and amended. Yes, this was a bit of extra work, which is why many managers and business owners simply pursue a quick fix, ignore the lesson, and move on. But we chose not to look away because that would limit and impair our growth. It's always a good idea to document how you want tasks handled, which then becomes a starting point for your internal processes and procedures.

Every business operator has preferences regarding the tools they like to use to become more efficient. Personally, being somewhat of a scatter-brain personality type, I am a big fan of simple, complete, very short, condensed, one-page spreadsheets that summarize the status of each project. I am a very visual person that needs to see all the data in one place, as opposed to shuffling though a bunch of pages.

As your company grows, you will constantly be coming up with personalized designs of spreadsheets that accommodate your management style. Eventually, as you become unable to rely on your memory alone, you will depend on these sources of information. These reports establish a footprint that will clearly convey to everyone involved what you want done and how you want it done. Thankfully, we have access to all sorts of electronic devices that can make this easier, so you now can share information as much as you want to the people you want in *real time*. Those forms and checklists become the best communication tools as your team expands.

More systems lead to less human error.

Written agreements between developers and the contractors performing each individual duty are necessary and should be executed in as much detail as possible to prevent misunderstandings. As part of this process, you should consider every scenario and every miniscule part of the work expected to be completed, including contingencies and unpredictable circumstances. You must ensure that it is carefully drafted and that it describes the scope of work in detail and not just in general or you will end up paying extra for items that you assumed were included in the contract.

Ask questions about what the subcontractor is including and what they are not and request a breakdown of the components that make up the proposal.
The same goes for contracts between developers and general contractors for the construction of entire homes. There must be a clause that allows the developer to monitor and ensure payments made to all the individual companies working on your project. There is often misallocation of funds by inexperienced or

Today, for example, amongst many other systems, when we get a property under contract, we have a development checklist we use to confirm which tasks have been done. This, along with many other informative reports, are contained in a shared drive. When items are completed, the appropriate person approves them. These checklists help you, as the business owner, monitor progress and timeframes. Eventually, you'll also want to invest in software to help manage the business, particularly for things like purchase orders. Initially, purchase order (PO) systems are not crucial, but once you reach a certain volume, meaning a dozen or so homes, it becomes imperative. Traditional bookkeeping software does not have the capability to manage or keep up with budgets and payments for multiple projects. It is very easy to lose track of all the purchases you have made for a particular house, but when you have a purchase order system, any expenses associated with a particular address can be programed, recorded, easily categorized, and filed away for reference later. Purchase order systems alert you to who you have already paid, how much, and whether it was a partial payment, a progress payment, or a final payment. It also tells you how on budget you are, or how over budget you may be before it's too late to rectify. This will be your most important weapon against accidentally over-paying or double paying for things.

Setting up online systems to track your progress on everything from permits to construction to budgeting helps you stay on track to finish and close by your deadline. But this will happen gradually over time, as you recognize the need to keep better track of various aspects of the home design and construction process.

bad-intentioned contractors where you may advance money for a specific item and your funds end up going to something else or to a project that may not even be yours. With the correct contract in place describing everything agreed upon, if an unanticipated event occurs, the parties have an "out," or a clear reason to renegotiate the contract with each other in the event of default. Without it, however, parties are stuck in a dispute without progress at the job site.

CHAPTER 5

Financial Projections and Home Selections

Staying in business once you're up and running is the next challenge. Your ability to build a profitable company depends on a variety of talents, one of them being the art of finance. For this reason, it is time to jump from preliminary to actual budgets, and for that we need to make some decisions. Let's start by differentiating the costs to build each home from what it costs to operate your company. Meaning, you need to master building-related expenses separately from the behind-the-scenes expenses related to everything else, from your office space to your attorney's and accountant's fees to office supplies, website hosting, administrative labor, and marketing materials, to name just a few.

There are two basic business costs: 1) variable, also called cost of goods sold (COGS), house related, or direct costs, meaning the design, materials, and building. And then there's 2) your fixed costs, also called operating costs, non-related, or indirect costs, which are the back-of-the-house finance and administration. When my

FINANCIAL PROJECTIONS AND HOME SELECTIONS

brother and I started Tricon, he was the architect, builder, and designer, and I was the finance investor/administrator who took care of the business side of things. But unless you have a partner who brings specialized skills to the company, you're going to need to be able to attend to both aspects of your business. Neither one can be ignored.

Nearly all businesses have two parts—the production side and the administrative side. This is not unique to home building. In fact, several businesses that I have invested in over the years failed because the founder lacked one of these two skills. In most cases, the founder was an expert in his specialty and a superb technician, but he had no clue how to manage a business. Dealing with lenders, managing resources, tracking business expenses, collections, calculating payroll, reporting tax withholding, paying rent, training and managing people, or estimating raw material costs turned out to be weaknesses that caused the demise of several companies.

This task is not as complicated, but it's often skipped when all you need is to spend a little time figuring it out. Then you'll want to make use of a budget to help you identify and manage all of the tangible costs of building homes, as well as the unbillable administrative costs associated with running the business.

Two basic types of costs and expenses

Although there are dozens of different types of costs associated with owning a business and building a house, technically they fall into two main categories, which in the accounting world are simply called *fixed* or *variable*.

Fixed costs, *as mentioned previously, are also referred to as operating costs, non-related, or indirect costs.*

Your fixed costs are typically part of your overhead, meaning expenses required to stay in business whether you build anything or not. These costs are not directly related to the construction itself but to the behind-the-scenes expenses such as mileage on your car, bank charges, software subscriptions, general liability insurance, a bookkeeper, a copier, and the paper and toner cartridges for the copier. These are some of the costs required to support the business's operation.

Some expenses associated with selling a finished home are unnecessary and others are essential. Staging, in my opinion, is one I would consider essential, because homes that are staged, meaning they have furniture and home décor in place, sell faster and for more money. Yes, it will cost some money for the design services and the rental of the furniture and other pieces, but staging can mean the difference between selling a home and not.

I know this because my team and I frequently walk our buyers through an empty home and then walk them through another that was fully furnished. They would then tell us they preferred the staged home because it felt more comfortable, brighter, even more spacious. Yet the truth was both homes were exactly the same, minus the décor. That's how important staging is, so don't skip that expense.

These are called fixed expenses because they need to be paid whether you sold ten houses this month or none, whether you have revenue or not this month, so it's always smart to keep them as low as possible when you're starting out. The higher your overhead, the more pressure you'll have to sell every house at a substantial profit, which isn't always possible. If you can operate out of your dining room at the start, try to save every penny you can.

Variable costs are also called cost of goods sold (COGS), house-related or direct costs, and to make it even more fun, in the construction world, a more technical name for this expense is Work In Progress (WIP).

Your variable costs change based on the home or homes that you're building. These are strictly related to building your product. For example, what you pay for land is very likely going to differ based on where you're buying. Whether there is a structure on the land or not will dictate if you have demo costs and whether it's already subdivided the way you need it or not will determine if you need a re-plat. Those types of costs will vary from project to project.

Likewise, what you decide to spend on flooring, landscaping, lighting, appliances, etc. will also change depending on the size, specifications, and location of the home you're constructing. Most of these costs are determined separately for each home. You will only buy materials when you build your home and you will only buy insurance for the specific homes that you are building. These material costs will fluctuate depending on the selections you make and how many houses you build, which is why they are variable, or changing, rather than ongoing and fixed, such as the salaries you pay your full-time employees.

Let's go a little further in breaking down these variable (house-related) costs, which all fall into a big group called work in progress (WIP), also known as cost of goods sold (COGS).

The three main categories of WIP are:

Raw land: Lots that you own and which are waiting to be developed.

Lot inventory: Fully developed lots ready to be built on (also called shovel-ready lots).

Home inventory: Homes under construction; they are currently being built.

If we dig deeper, which we will in the next chapter, land and homes themselves each also have two separate categories of costs, which are divided into soft costs and hard costs. When you develop a lot, before you even set foot on it, there is a list of intangible costs associated with your project that are necessary. These are referred to as soft costs. Then there is a list of hard expenses, which represent the actual work that will take place at the site to prepare the lot for a house to be built. Something very similar happens with the house, where you will also have to start spending money on a list of items before you actually break ground, meaning your soft costs. Then, of course, you move on to the tangible hard costs.

Needless to say, budgets differ based on whether you're building one house or several, as well as whether you are building on an existing street or creating an entirely new community, which would require additional steps.

Picking a style and specialty to start

Persistence and dedication help you build a business, but taste and allowances will help you perfect the process of accurately deciding what type of homes you want to build. You must take time figuring out what styles or locations you most appreciate. Are you drawn to modern architecture, or do you prefer Victorian homes, for example? Do you love the farmhouse look or are you more a fan of Mediterranean houses? Are you inspired by warehouses that are turned into lofts or do you like traditional, single-family houses?

There's no wrong answer here, really, as long as you like some mainstream styles. If you love a more out-of-the-box style that you've developed yourself or that would be considered extreme by most buyers, that's great, but you may have trouble selling them. (I'm picturing buildings like the Flintstone House in Hillsborough, California, which is a replica of the 1970s cartoon home, for example. Very cool design, but not your typical dwelling.) So, feel free to design your own personal home in that style. But to build a profitable business, unless you are building an entire community with its own environment, you must limit your style choices to those that are already present in the area where you're planning to do business. And, to start, choose just one that you will offer buyers.

Eventually, you can build any style home, but at the start, you need to build an identity and a reputation in your community for one type of home. I often use the analogy of a restaurant. Eventually you can have a chain consisting of several types of eateries, but at the beginning, get good at one type of cooking before you expand. I recommend you apply that same thinking to home building: master one style that you prefer before you move on to building other styles.

The biggest reason for mastering one style is that you will learn all the ins and outs of that particular type of structure. You'll learn about the typical costs, where you can save money and where you can't, who the best contractors are for the type of work you need, and what buyers of those types of home are looking for. Get good at one style before switching. Otherwise, you will constantly be on a learning curve, which will likely impact how profitable your business can become.

Design choices

The choices you make regarding the design of your houses go beyond exterior appearance and footprint and also involve:

- Price point
- Square footage
- Layout – floor plan
- Target audience
- Specifications
- Finishes
- Amenities
- Exterior features

As you make these choices in your houses, you'll want to keep in mind the surrounding neighborhood and nearby homes, so that your home blends in with what is already there or that is in the process of being built. You don't want your house to stand out like a sore thumb; that's counterproductive to selling it quickly and making a profit. Also, ask yourself who are you building for and what is on their wish list?

Also keep in mind that trends in interior design change fairly rapidly. When I started building, the preferred colors were dark, so we used a lot of dark mahogany stain on the floors and cabinets, black granite countertops, and dark tile because that's what homeowners preferred. Today when you walk into a house with a darker color scheme, it feels dated. What's trendy right now is lighter natural colors, which will presumably change in the next five to ten years as tastes shift. We're seeing earthy or light-colored cabinets rather than dark wood.

Your goal in designing your homes should always be to appeal to the masses. Unless your plan is to pre-sell your house and have a buyer locked in (who will then dictate color choices), you want to make the interior as neutral as possible.

> Whatever your house's exterior appearance, do your best to make the inside trendy and timeless. Whether the house is modern or Mediterranean or traditional on the outside, once your buyer steps through the front door, you want to show them how flexible the floor plan is. They want reassurance that they will be able to furnish and decorate the interior however they choose. That means that, unless the neighborhood consists of extreme Tudor-style homes, you probably don't want lots of wood beams running across your ceilings or stone archways. At the same time, you also probably want to avoid sunken living rooms, posts that break up rooms, and oversized built-ins. Those types of design features can limit the size and type of furniture your buyers can use, which will limit your pool of buyers.

Learning what's trending

For those of you who feel you have little to no decorating talent, or zero sense of style, I recommend that you hire a trained interior designer to put together a full set of selections for your houses before they are built. Each package will address every detail related to fixtures and finishes, like stain colors, hardware, lighting, appliances, brands, serial numbers, as well as where to buy each item. This shopping list will make it easier for you to make such decisions, without having to research and choose each and every item that a house requires. Eventually you will become more familiar with the selections that are more popular and which correspond to the product that you are building.

Fortunately, there are people who offer this service to builders for a flat fee. If you don't already have a contact, visit your nearest design center or ask your cabinet manufacturer, stone, tile, or lighting distributor for some names of local designers, and they should be able to refer you to someone who can assist you with this. You don't necessarily need a full-blown decorator or professional interior designer; they are often more expensive.

To start, you'll provide the basic description of your project (house or development), the style, floor plan, and price point. The consultant will then generate selections based on your criteria and general allowances. You will then review the package, make any comments or modifications, and after a couple of rounds, you should come up with the perfect set of final selections for you to approve for the home you're building.

If you have knowledge in this field and want to save some money, or you are feeling adventurous and want to make these decisions on your own, that's perfectly fine, too. I, for instance, can rely on my wife Adriana—who immersed herself in the design world—to make these choices for our priciest and most luxurious homes. In this case, unless you go after more official training, you'll need to be familiar with what's trending now. That's easy to discover. Instagram is a great source of design ideas, plus watching videos or TV shows about real estate, reading home design magazines, looking at home design websites online, and touring homes being built in your area that are selling can provide a great education. There is so much information available to help guide your selections.

Finishes—meaning the choices you make to create a cosmetically pleasing house, such as your color schemes, floors, countertops, backsplashes, cabinets, doors, handrails, hardware, fixtures, appliances, etc.—are extremely important to the appeal and marketability of a home. There are several components that make a good selections package. They must be trendy and up to date, appeal to a majority of consumers—and not just a limited niche market—reflect budgets in line with your price point, and agree with the style and vision of your floor plan. The selections package itself should include details like sizes, measurements, serial and model numbers, dimensions, brands and manufacturers, unit prices or price-per-foot, availability, as well as links to websites or information regarding where to purchase each item. It must all be so complete and self-explanatory that your contractors will understand every aspect without additional instruction, including technical descriptions that contain everything down to the grout and patterns to be used for the installation of your tile and backsplash.

In other words, there should be very little left to interpretation and to the imagination of the contractors who will do the actual work. You don't want to leave any margin for human error, which can cause delays and costly mistakes.

The best approach to figuring out what is likely to work best in a house you're building is to start by examining the macro trends. That is, what are the bigger home design trends nationwide? Your city may be ahead of or behind the national trends, but get a general sense of what buyers today prefer. The preferred colors, styles, and materials evolve, but each decade generally has prominent design elements the times were known for. (Remember the popular avocado green of the 1960s or the variety of crazy wallpaper patterns?)

Next, start narrowing your scope to your city. Look at local home-related publications and watch videos of home interiors that are on the market *in your area* to see what's popular. Then narrow your scope even further to your neighborhood or your street. What do other homes look like? What features do they have? What are the color schemes of the updated spaces? And most importantly, what's selling?

Yes, you want your home to be eye-catching and noteworthy, but for the right reasons. You don't want it to be the only bright-colored home on a street of pastels, for example, or the only bungalow on a street of ultra-modern properties. Nor do you want it to be the home with solid wood doors when all of the other homes in your price range have hollow core, stamped hardboard, or molded composite laminate. In that case, you would have overspent on those amenities; buyers interested in that neighborhood are not expecting certain high-priced items. Be sure that your $300,000 doesn't feature amenities or brands that are more commonly found in $3 million homes, or vice versa.

That is the challenge at the start of each home project—assessing what the standards are for each fixture and finish. When we started building in a new subdivision or neighborhood, one of the first questions we needed to answer was, "What does this house have to contain to be marketable at the projected sales price?" We needed to understand what components made sense for that neighborhood and price. For example, based on the other houses there, could we get away with laminate wood floors or would we need Brazilian walnut, or even a custom engineered European brand name? Does the house need crown molding? Would it make sense to include a double oven or a dishwasher? Does it need to be a La Cornue or can it be Kenmore?

You need to ask yourself, based on your research, what type of house do you want to build and offer to your customer? What would sell well in the location you're looking at? What is a conservative price-per-square-foot that you could sell the house for once built?

Once you have those answers, then you work backwards to make decisions about what buyers will expect the house to have. You create a checklist of all the things the home needs in order to sell fast. Then you review each line item and decide what is essential, for the style and price point you're building, and what can be eliminated. For example, can you use ceramic tile or do you need to invest in quartz or marble? Can you use prefabricated cabinets or do they need to be custom-built by a carpenter? What kind of lighting is necessary? Can you use a six-inch can light instead of a pricier four-inch? Does the insulation need to be batt-fiberglass, blown, or even foam? These types of decisions will be dictated by where the house is geographically (air conditioning is a must in Texas, for example, but may be optional in Maine) and the selling price you're aiming for.

It's very easy to overspend in relation to your asking price or the area you're building in. Newer builders sometimes believe that because they invested more money in building a house, they will be able to charge more for it when it's done. That is a big misconception and they are generally wrong. If you invest, say, $400,000 in a house in a neighborhood where the average home sells for $250,000, it is extremely unlikely that you'll be able to convince a buyer to go up in price by that much. Nor will a bank be likely to lend a buyer the money for the purchase, given that it is overpriced for the market and without previous comparable sales. The market is what it is—you can't dictate what a house will sell for, no matter how hard you try. So, don't put more features and finishes in than your price point allows.

CHAPTER 6

Budgets—Finding Money and Allocating It

Now that we have a better idea of what a house like yours can sell for in the location it is in, with the features and amenities you have planned, it's time to put together some budgets that will help you confirm what you should spend in order to make money.

Let's get back to the three categories of WIP, or COGS, which we previously learned to be raw land, developed land, and home inventory.

Land development costs

Land development consists of converting a piece of raw land into a buildable lot(s). The process of developing land will incur soft costs and hard costs and there is no exact rule or science to split the two types. One builder may think of demolition or architectural fees as hard costs because they add value to their project, while another may place it under the soft costs category because they consider them prep work and not part of the infrastructure of the new development. Either approach is fine. So, let's not get too caught up in categorizing them as much as understanding the general picture. What's most important is ensuring that all related expenses are covered and accounted for, regardless of where you categorize them. There are too many variables to consider, but in general, here is a list of some basic items commonly referred to as soft versus hard costs as a reference:

Land Development Soft Costs

    Civil Engineering
    Soil Tests/Compaction Tests
    Impact Fees
    Phase I Environmental Site Assessment (ESA)
    Plan and Profile/Drainage Plans
    Replat Cost
    Common Area Agreement
    Plan Runner/Administrative
    Civil Permits

Land Development Hard Costs

    Structural Demo and Tree Removal
    Site clearing, Scraping, Leveling
    Temporary Fencing
    Security or Cameras
    Permanent Exterior Perimeter Fence
    Entrance Gates
    Entrance Signs
    Construction Pads/Select Fil
    Plumbing Undergrounds
    Gas Lines
    Electrical Undergrounds

BUDGETS—FINDING MONEY AND ALLOCATING IT

Streets (private street or shared drive)
Underground Electric/Gas/Internet Installation
Sidewalk, Entry Walkway, Handicap Ramp, Parking Space
Culvert Pipes
Retention Wall for Perimeter
Construction of Pond/Detention/Labor/Wall Rental
Excavation of Pond
Concrete for Pond/Detention
Pond Stairs and Fencing
Landscaping—Frontage and Common Areas
SWPPP and SWQ Bond
Topographic Survey and GPS
Staking Lots by Surveyor
Concrete Pump and Other Equipment Rental
Master Water Meters—Water/Sewer Taps and Permits
Cluster Mailboxes
Street Lighting

During this part of the project, your civil engineer will play the most important role. He or she will help you design your site, provide you with options as to how the property could be split, the number of lots and proposed dimensions of each to fit your homes, drainage, utilities, access, amenities, and so on. This design will guide the entire process of investigation, defining the parameters and requirements to develop your land. After a sequence of questions and answers, once the development has been agreed upon under your local town's or city's guidelines, the engineer will proceed to complete a set of civil plans that will describe in detail the subdivision you plan to build. After a few rounds of comments and revisions by the approving entities, you should be granted your civil permit, at which time you may begin the actual work on site. As we mentioned before, if the civil engineer has a good working relationship with your architect, this is a big advantage, because it will allow for a smooth level of communication between these two critical areas.

Keep in mind that if you purchase one or more shovel-ready lot(s), or a single-family lot facing an existing and already fully developed street, where you plan to build one home on each of those lots, your development costs should be minimal. The bulk of development budgets apply to properties that are not ready to be built on. And the bigger the lot and the more homes in the development, the higher the development costs.

If you are developing land, technically you could say that you will break ground twice. The first stage is referred to as civil work—it requires its own separate permit and it represents breaking ground by building the infrastructure of the lots. Stage 2 is referred to as "vertical construction," meaning breaking ground on the construction of the actual homes.

Until you obtain your approved civil permit, you can't yet begin getting official proposals and executing the work at the site. The contractors who will do the work on-site need to see the exact specifications of the development in order to provide accurate proposals, and you won't have this until your permit has been approved. This is the point at which your hard development costs begin. Infrastructure will be created and installed to prepare the lots to build homes on them. Your development costs are everything that occur up until you break ground on the house (vertical construction).

In general, when you add your total development costs to your land purchase price, they shouldn't exceed an amount that you would feel comfortable paying if you were to purchase a shovel-ready lot. How much you pay for your land can determine how much flexibility you have with your development budget.

There are two ways to go about developing your land. The first option is for you to hire a turnkey contractor who will obtain the individual prices for all the different items involved on the list of hard costs and you will basically be offered a flat fee for the work to be done. The second option is for you to act as the general contractor and to go out and get the individual items priced out and coordinate everything yourself. Both options have advantages: doing it yourself may take more time and effort but once you're experienced enough, you can have more control over schedules and costs. A general contractor may have relationships that could also get the work done for less than you could and help you avoid all the headaches. Price things both ways and see which option suits you best.

In both cases, the development will have to be built precisely according to every detail spelled out on your civil permits.

Construction budget

Assuming that you now have a full set of permitted construction home plans, you can now request quotes for your hard costs.

The budget associated with the construction of houses also has the two groups of soft and hard costs.

You may hear builders talk of "frontloaders" with respect to houses. Frontloaders are typically narrow homes with an attached garage on the front of them or with alley access to avoid the need for a wide driveway (also described as row houses or shotgun houses). These homes fit on lots with small footprints. They are normally facing an existing public or private street. Frontloaders are often confused with townhomes, which are not the same. What separates a townhome from a single-family home is the fact that townhomes are connected to each other (two or more) by common walls. Essentially, you could have a set of frontloading single-family homes, often called row houses, but once they are attached to each other by a sharing wall, they are considered townhomes because you are now sharing ownership of a structure.

In preparing a *soft cost* construction budget, you will consider all of the items that take place prior to breaking ground (see list below):

- ✦ Survey
- ✦ Appraisals
- ✦ Architectural Plans
- ✦ Structural Engineering

- Soil Samples
- Loan Origination Fees
- Closing Costs
- Construction Permits
- Plan Runner and Administrative Expenses
- Financing Interest/Carrying Costs
- Property Taxes
- Sales Costs and Commissions

Some soft costs continue to accrue even after you break ground, such as carrying costs, property taxes, maintenance, and utilities.

As for the *hard cost* construction budget, you can think through all of the elements from the ground up, literally. These include costs such as:

- Forms for Foundation
- Foundation and Driveways
- Framing
- Roofing
- Plumbing
- HVAC
- Electrical
- Low Voltage and Alarm System
- Temporary Security for the Job Site
- Siding
- Stucco
- Masonry
- Windows
- Exterior Doors
- Interior Doors
- Garage Doors
- Front Door
- Fireplace
- Insulation

- Drywall
- Paint
- Cabinets and Hardware
- Metal Works
- Glass and Mirrors
- Wood Floors and Carpeting
- Tile
- Countertops
- Trim
- Millwork
- Trees and Landscaping
- Appliances
- Gutters
- Gates and Fences
- Trash Pickup
- Cleaning Services
- Extras/Aftermarket (Pools, Wine Cellars, Elevators, Decks, Garage Apartments, Shutters/Blinds, Outdoor Kitchens, Steam Rooms, Electronic Equipment, Sound Systems, Wallpaper, Electric Gates)

Although you will ask for quotes from contractors for each piece of the building puzzle, it is also useful to think of them in terms of percentage completed when looking at your cash outflow, because that is how lenders approach construction draws. Meaning, as different parts of the house are built, your lender, the bank, will approve a payout to you based on the percentage of the house that has been completed and release that specific portion of your loan. So, for example, the bank may set aside ten percent of the construction budget for the framing and four percent for the foundation. That is how much of the total loan has been allocated for you to receive as you finish those components of the building.

However, in some cases, the breakdown of what you've spent on those components may be slightly different from what the bank is allowing for those items. For example, the bank may be ready to release ten percent of the total after they've confirmed that framing has been done, but it's possible that the framing only cost you eight percent of your budget. Or maybe it cost you eleven percent. Don't worry too much about it as long as your expenses are matching up to the actual budget you set up for yourself. Not all banks work with your exact same percentages, they have their own formats. By the end of the project, the bank will have released 100 percent of the amount you borrowed, which should cover your entire project.

What adds more complexity and makes some of this budgeting tricky is that not all bids are identical. Some of your contractors may include different items, fees, brands, and quality of products than others in their quotes. You'll want to make sure someone is taking care of all the necessary expenses, and that you are neither being billed twice for them nor not including them at all, therefore miscalculating your true costs. For example, one contractor may include permits, insurance, equipment rental, and trash hauling, while others may not. Some may even include the utilities during construction, and others won't.

Sometimes bids will come in that seem high at first glance, but when you look closely, you can see that the contractor had included costs that you hadn't expected them to, or perhaps they come much better recommended with higher ratings. You'll want to take everything into consideration, because the cheapest bid is not necessarily always the best choice.

Asking what costs are covered is also a way to begin the conversation with contractors about their bids, especially if they were higher than anticipated. Although the quotes you receive should be extremely detailed, asking, "Can we walk through what your proposal consists of, because I would like to better understand what you are and are not including. Can you explain it to me?" is a great way to clear up any confusion. This also makes sure you're comparing apples to apples as far as quotes go. Meaning, you can factor in extra expenses the contractor is planning to pay.

It really doesn't matter who is paying for them as long as you have a list of all of your budget line items and know who is responsible for each one. It's important to be sure that none are missed, so that you aren't hit with an unexpected bill after the fact that you thought someone else was paying.

A budget and an allowance are two different but similar terms you should be familiar with. You have your total budget, which is what you plan to spend on the house, then you have your budget categories or subcategories (same thing), which represent what you anticipate spending for each subcategory of the different parts and components of construction. That's money you have allocated, which you will then pay vendors and contractors for labor and materials.

Allowances are what you allocate to spend on the individually selected items within an expense subcategory. For example, you will assign how much you spend as an "allowance" for light fixtures, which happen to be a small part of your total electrical budget. Allowances are a great point of reference that break down budgets into smaller pieces, guiding you as to what you are able to spend on each component of each phase. It zooms in on specifics, ensuring that no item is forgotten, and if you go over budget, you can easily identify the cause. An analogy would be your paycheck, which represents your total budget, and your grocery shopping list is a subcategory of your budget; let's use $100 for the week to make this simple. This is where allowances come in. You will take that $100 budget and allow $20 of it for breakfast items, $30 for lunches, and $50 for dinners. That should guide your grocery shopping for the week. However, if you simply walk down the food aisles and put random things in your grocery cart, you may end up spending all your money on a bunch of snacks and a steak, leaving very little to eat for the remainder of the week.

This is particularly relevant if you're building a custom home, in which case you will provide your buyer with a certain amount of money to spend on items such as kitchen cabinets, plumbing fixtures, hardware, bathroom tile, flooring, or countertops. If they decide to pay for an upgrade that costs more than their allowance, they are responsible for paying the difference. So, if their flooring allowance is, say, $5/square foot and they really want an option that costs $10/square foot, they can certainly choose that, but then you will bill them the additional $5/square foot as part of the cost of the home.

At the core of these calculations are the takeoffs. Takeoffs consist of the details and actual count (quantity) of materials needed for each stage of the construction process, based on the specific measurements for the house being built. Based on your construction plans, the person pricing the different stages of the process will have to create an itemized inventory of the number of units of each and every type of construction material required to build the house. The foundation, for example, consists of the square footage times the cost of concrete related to the specifications being used, the volume and density, and pounds-per-square-inch (PSI) specified, meaning the pressure that your concrete will need to tolerate. Effectively, you're calculating the number of units you'll need of any given item or the square footage times a cost-per-square-foot to build it. The same is done for most things, such as frame, roof, plumbing, electrical, sheetrock, tile flooring, etc.

You can create your own list of takeoffs for a particular house plan, or you can have them done by a third party. There are companies that will create them for you.

Just as in your development phase, there are two ways to come up with a construction budget associated with the house you're planning to build. This will depend on the type of builder you are. One way is to develop a full set of construction plans and then price out each component individually to get your total. That is how it is done if your company is serving as the general contractor.

In this case, you would basically photocopy each section of the plans, from plumbing to electrical to structural, etc., and hand the relevant plan over to the contractor to price out. They will do the calculations and quote you a price for their work, which you then build into your construction budget. If you like and trust their estimates and they can guarantee the quoted cost, you don't need to calculate takeoffs at all.

Once you have quotes in-hand from all of the subcontractors bidding on the many sections of the house you're planning to build, you're in a position to confirm your preliminary estimates.

Another way, if you're working with a turnkey company, is to hand over all of the approved plans to receive a price-per-foot quote for the entire house, based on the specifications. In this case, the company will provide you with allowances for each item requiring a selection, such as for tile, carpentry, plumbing and lighting fixtures, hardware, landscaping, appliances, and flooring, for example, while specifying how much each allowance is.

While you might be excited by some of the low bids you receive, as I mentioned earlier, the cheapest option is not always the best. By no means am I against going with the lowest bid, but make sure that it's not due to a company's lack of experience, inaccurate calculations, or poor craftsmanship. You don't want to be working with contractors who are more worried about speed than quality.

Nor do you want to put too much pressure on your contractors to cut their prices. Your best option is to be fair. You want to make the numbers work on your budget, but you also want them to make some money, too, or they won't be in business much longer, and neither will you.

Unless you work pretty consistently with certain tradespeople and they know they can count on you for a certain amount of work each month, don't expect to pay rock-bottom prices. Over time, you can rehire contractors you like who do good work and replace those whose work you think could have been better. Little by little, you build your core team of contractors while also improving your cost structure, your workmanship, your timing, and your relationships in the industry.

Your surveys, which I briefly covered during our due diligence section and will continue expanding on later, are very important, including your forms survey, which we will discuss in more detail later on. The forms survey is the one indicating the location of your foundation's perimeter. There are many aspects of building a house that can go wrong. Many things you can correct after the fact, but you cannot fix the location of your foundation once it's been poured. So, before you break ground, have your surveyor go and mark the property, stake it, and then survey the wood forms. This is basically where the house will sit.

There are frequently discrepancies of a few inches here or there, which you have to rectify before you pour the concrete for the foundation. Some information in your construction plans is computer-generated while other items are manually entered, like window and door types, schedules, amounts, and measurements. It helps if you review and verify each page of your construction plans. Because once that's in place, there's no going back. And by the way, surveyors and foundation companies do make mistakes sometimes. Cross-referencing everyone's findings to match your plans is a must. So, dot your i's and cross your t's and do not pour your foundation until you've carefully completed and examined your forms survey. To articulate the importance of this step, no matter how many dozens of homes we had going up simultaneously, regardless of how many other important issues were happening, my brother Tristan would sometimes delegate different areas of the construction process *except this one*. With absolutely no room for mistakes, he would closely monitor every step personally until foundations were accurately and successfully poured.

Pricing per-square-foot

There are actually two square-foot measurements made within houses: 1) air-conditioned and 2) total living space. Your total living space includes balconies, decks, and outdoor living areas, such as roofed outdoor patios and outdoor kitchens. Because there is a potentially big difference between the interior square footage of the house and the total square footage of the living space, you'll want to verify how your contractors are calculating their bids. For example, you might have a home that has 3,000 square feet of air-conditioned space and another 1,500 square feet outdoors. And if a lighting or interior painting subcontractor is trying to bill you based on a 4,500-square-foot house, you'll want to question that price.

Speaking of outdoor living spaces, you should always consider these areas when creating budgets. Fancy front elevation "façades," balconies, decks, porches, outdoor kitchens, pools, long or circular driveways, gardens, and large front or side yards quickly escalate your cost-per-foot without making the house any bigger. Styles can make or break budgets! Always be conscientious of the non-air-conditioned amenities and price them separately to see if they are worth it.

Preparing a loan request

Although banks have different missions, operating philosophies, approval committees, and lending processes, when all is said and done, most require the same set of documents to be considered for a construction loan. These typically include:

+ Three years of personal tax returns
+ Three years of business taxes, if you currently own and operate your own company
+ A personal financial statement summarizing all of your assets and liabilities
+ A business financial statement if you currently own and operate your own company
+ Your incorporation documents
+ A floor plan of the house you intend to build
+ Specifications and selections of the house
+ A site plan
+ A survey

might get five percent of the total once the foundation is down and another ten percent once the framing is done, and so on through the whole construction process. Every time you finish something, you'll need to contact the bank, submit a draw request describing the work completed, and they will send an inspector to verify it. Once the inspection is completed, the bank will fund you after the fact, so you need to have money to put down up-front to pay for the work being done, unless your contractors have the ability to float you while you get reimbursed by the bank. This is rarely the case and even if they can afford to do so, they may not be willing until you have a long-standing relationship with each of them.

How to obtain your first loan

The first time you attempt anything in business, it's difficult. That's true with respect to finding land as well as obtaining your first construction loan. Lenders are reluctant to give you money because you have no track record. They aren't confident you will be skilled enough to build a business and pay the loan back. So, when you start knocking on bank doors in search of your first loan, expect that it may take multiple attempts. You may have to knock on several doors and be rejected a few times before you find someone willing to take a chance on you.

Don't get discouraged, because each lending officer who turns down your request to borrow money is a source of information. When your loan request is declined, ask why. What is it that your application is missing or overlooking? I always ask questions like: Would you consider a loan for a smaller amount? Would you be more comfortable if I built in a different neighborhood? Would you approve it if I put up more equity, or perhaps an additional guarantor? What if I hired a well-recognized architect or general contractor? What if I move my personal and business operating accounts here? Find out, then revise your request and keep improving your approach for that or for the next lender. You can always try to adapt if you learn what the objections are, rather than to simply take no for an answer. Also, they might be rejecting you based on reasons not related to you, but to internal policies regarding their current appetite for those particular types of loans.

That first loan request is the most challenging, because you don't have the basics in place. You either don't have a financial history or you don't have experience in the business. And you certainly don't have relationships with bankers that might lead someone to take a chance. Building a relationship with a banker should be something you start working on now. In my experience, cold calling or introducing yourself is not very effective. Loan officers are not necessarily thrilled about discussing business with the first random person who walks in without some sort of referral. Being introduced by someone you know is always a much better proposition. Ask everyone you know if they can recommend you to a banker.

Most new builders don't have established business banking relationships, but if you happen to, you're ahead of the game. If you have existing bank accounts in one place and a longstanding history, you may be considered financially capable and may qualify for the loan based on your personal track record and financial strength rather than your construction experience. You should always present all your qualifications, whether this means financial strength, experience in this field, or entrepreneurship skills in any other industry. Everything counts.

However, unless you fall into this category, I wouldn't waste time setting up appointments with national banks. They don't like these start-up deals because they don't understand them. Even if they do, they're not crazy about interim-builder financing because of the amount of work involved.

Community and regional banks and credit unions, on the other hand, are your best bet. They are interested in serving members of their community. Local entrepreneurs should always start with local banks, which have a stated mission to support the growth of the community in which they operate. Credit unions are also a possibility, although they have different underwriting guidelines and procedures, but if you're already a member of a credit union, start there.

Now, if you have no significant experience, no banking relationships, no industry contacts, no major assets or collateral, and very little cash to show for, this will be a challenge but you're not alone. So don't worry because that's exactly where I started. In cases like this we need creativity. I could tell you that the best way to overcome this challenge would be to go to work for another builder, gain experience, and save some money, but you probably don't want to hear that, so let's think of another way.

If you already own a home or have a savings account, that means you probably have good credit. If that's the case, you could always apply for a second home loan and use it to build that first "spec" house. If you don't have much money and no home, but decent credit, we can also use that to our advantage. That's the situation I effectively found myself in initially. Banks didn't want to lend me money to build a spec home, or a house that may not sell as planned, but if I could reclassify it as a pre-sold home, that would put me in a much different position.

I didn't own a home when we built that first $100,000 bungalow, but I had $7,500 to invest in buying a lot. Although the bank did not want to fund a spec home that we would build for us to later attempt to sell, I thought of the idea of presenting the loan request as a custom job already sold to myself. In other words, I didn't ask for a loan to build a spec home, I requested a loan to build a home for me to live in. To my surprise, they were willing to do that. I qualified for that amount and committed to buying the home by accepting to convert that construction loan to a permanent mortgage once the house was finished. From a business perspective, the risk was lower. And there it was—our first construction loan.

The terms didn't prevent me from selling it while it was being built, the bank just wanted a plan B in the event that it didn't sell. They wanted something to fall back on, meaning a mortgage in my name that would pay off the construction loan. This was a pretty safe proposition for all of us, because if we couldn't sell it, the worst-case scenario was that I would own it and live in it. But as the story goes, the house sold prior to completing it and everyone was happy. And guess what? We now had a résumé as successful builders! We could officially claim to have that famous track record that everyone demanded.

After we completed our first build, it became easier to get the next one, then even easier to get the third, and so on. Soon enough we had more lines of credit than we knew what to do with.

Another possible tactic is to ask any family or friends who have strong finances or excellent credit record if they would be willing to back you. Meaning, they guarantee the loan with you. You could offer a commission or share of the profit in exchange for them taking that risk with you. Sure, that may seem scary at first, so you'll need to make it financially worth their while. The truth is that this is also an opportunity for them, which is how most enterprises begin. There is always risk, but they could also benefit from it. In a worst-case scenario, if the market shifts and you can't sell it, you can offer the exclusive right for them to take over the loan, transfer title to them *at your cost*, and they can keep it to either live in it or as a rental income property. Under this scenario you would have essentially worked for them for free, which shows a lot of commitment on your part. People with means are constantly looking for these types of opportunities from hard-working entrepreneurs.

Let's not forget that banks will only lend you a fraction of the project cost—seventy-five to eighty-five percent at best. So, you have to come up with the rest, which is where the equity investor comes in.

I'm sure you've heard of crowdfunding platforms, which exist to collect money for projects and causes, and there's always a possibility you could find a supporter there, but just know that they'll perform their own feasibility study. This requires you to go through a review process where they'll examine the details of your project, your plan of attack, proposed strategy, they will validate your numbers and schedules with a fine-tooth comb, verify your background, credit, management team, and other details. But unless you have the cash available yourself, the quickest and easiest source is going to be friends and family. People who know, like, and trust you are going to be much more willing to try to help you out than a stranger on GoFundMe. Especially if you're known to have good work ethics.

No lender will give you 100 percent of the project costs. There's really no way around it. You need to pull together the equity piece yourself.

Now, that twenty-five percent or so equity you'll need to close a deal with a bank isn't all that you should have at your disposal. The reality is that you're going to need more. In simple terms, banks lend you money for the more tangible aspects of the project, things that can somewhat be recovered if everything goes wrong. You need to be aware of those cash requirements that you'll need to find somewhere else. Those include things such as closing costs, a portion of the soft costs, property taxes, interest and carrying costs, your operating expenses, and most importantly, advances and deposits made to contractors for labor and materials to officially tie up their services. Since the bank pays you based on completion milestones, you won't get access to your money there until *after* the work has been done. And it won't get done if you can't pay your contractors a deposit to start.

There is no hard rule for how much of a cushion you should build up, and more is always better, but I'd guess that roughly another twelve percent of the total project cost on top of the bank's equity would be a good number to aim for. On a $400,000 house, that's an additional $50,000 you'd want to be able to access.

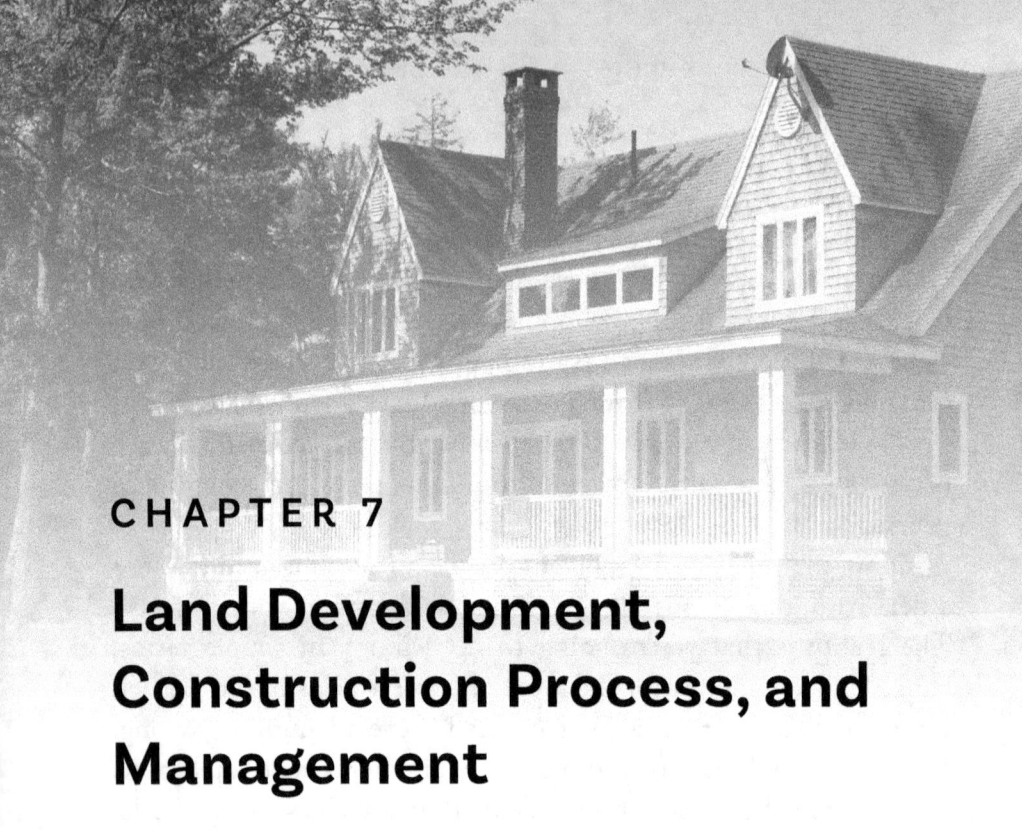

CHAPTER 7

Land Development, Construction Process, and Management

As stated before, land development involves the large-scale conversion of raw or undeveloped land into plots ready to be built on.

There are variations of this process based on how you plan to use the land. Preparing a piece of land to build a medical center, office buildings, industrial park, a shopping mall, an airport, a multifamily complex, or a single-family community each have slightly different steps and requirements. Being familiar with one type of building doesn't mean that you automatically know them all, so use caution before assuming you do.

Let's recap what the process of developing residential lots entails. Once you've determined that the property you selected is suitable to be subdivided and have homes built on it, meaning you have already conducted a full due diligence examination and feasibility study, you should have already begun the process of re-platting and permitting the land. Permitting consists of acquiring a civil permit, which is also known as a site development permit, although the steps required will vary based on location and the characteristics of the property. By this time, you have already met and discussed all the details with your civil engineer and with the corresponding city officials who provided the general guidelines.

This process will require the approval of many different local departments, including code enforcement, preliminary review, planning, utilities, plumbing, storm drainage, public works, engineering, traffic, utilities, infrastructure, and others. As part of your civil plans, you'll want to address everything that the development should incorporate in the site plan, including but not limited to:

- Access size and number of entry points
- Width and specifications of the streets and driveways
- Layout
- Setbacks
- Lot dimensions
- Drainage plans
- Detention or retention design and details
- How and where to connect to existing utilities
- Water lines
- Sewer/storm sewer lines
- Electricity lines
- Cable lines
- Necessary easements (where will they run and how wide)
- A design for all the underground lines and their acceptable slope according to depth and distance (plan and profile)
- Description and placement of all common areas
- Sidewalks
- Lighting
- Gates
- Fences

- ✦ Parking
- ✦ Fire hydrants and other fire department requirements
- ✦ Trees and landscaping
- ✦ Capacity and location of water and electrical meters
- ✦ Location of mailboxes
- ✦ Materials and specifications to be used for every component

Depending on your local rules, you should typically be able to start the process of obtaining your civil permits while you're simultaneously processing your re-plat, with the understanding that you won't get the final civil permit approved until you can show proof of your new recorded re-plat.

Once you have completed the permitting process, you may now begin actual work at the job site. It should all be performed exactly as dictated on the approved plans. Any change or variation will cause you to fail later inspections, so you need to pay close attention.

Your general contractor will price each and every item included in the plans so that you have an exact budget before breaking ground. When all of the work is completed, the development must pass a final inspection, at which time you officially have permitted developed building lots.

Survey work

Before we proceed, I want to emphasize again how critical surveys are and the role they play. Surveys are a crucial piece of this whole business because they serve as reference tools for everyone who is helping to build your house. The engineers, the architects, the city representatives, the appraiser, lenders, your construction crew, and even your neighbors who are affected by changes or inaccuracies—they will all rely on the data shown on your surveys to ensure you get the house you expect, precisely where you expect it on the lot.

Although I don't want to get off on too big a tangent about the basic background of land surveying, I think it would be useful for you to understand the early process of how parcels of land became what they are today. Imagine that at some point land was subdivided into very large chunks of hundreds, thousands, or even hundreds of thousands of acres. Those plats of land over time were gradually divided into smaller pieces, as portions of them were sold, granted, or inherited to multiple parties and then new sub-plats were created. As these smaller and smaller pieces of land changed ownership, new surveys for each piece—called a "re-plat"—were produced and recorded. Every time a "re-plat" is recorded, more detail, purpose, descriptions, utilization, and characteristics of the land are added to the record.

Land surveying is a very extensive subject with many types of them involved. Initially they are done to identify and outline the shape and the boundaries of a certain piece of land. A plat or a subdivision plat is a map that refers to the way a piece of land is subdivided into smaller lots or plots; it provides the macro view of your project. A survey is produced to outline the exact coordinates of each of those smaller lots that resulted from the re-plat. However, a survey, unlike a re-plat, also shows more detail regarding everything that sits on the lot or goes through the lot.

Another survey you'll want to look at is your topographic survey, which shows the altitudes or elevations of the land, including measurements in relation to the street or to the height of every point on the lot.

After your replat has been recorded, you'll need to request that your surveyor return to the property to re-survey the new individual lots that you created within the old boundary; remember that you just created new addresses by recording a new re-plat. Those new boundaries will need to be documented on the ground. The surveyor will stake the new corners of each of the new lots. Of course, next in line is your construction form survey, which we've already explained.

Next is your foundation survey, which is done to indicate exactly where the concrete was poured to confirm that the work was done correctly. The surveyor will actually come back *again* after the foundation is poured to measure and draw up the coordinates of where the new structure is placed. Many banks will want to see that updated drawing before releasing funds.

And, finally, your completed survey is done once the house is finished. Although it's too early to discuss this stage, it's worth mentioning while we're on this subject. This is typically ordered and purchased by the home buyer once the property goes under contract, as it is necessary for their records and required by the mortgage lender. Surveyors return to measure and record everything from the location of the house, the driveways, gates, fences, landscaping, trees (if requested), detached structures like garages or guest houses, setbacks, the placement of utility meters, and encroachments, to name a few. That completed survey is the final record of where everything is located inside the property boundaries.

There is so much to know about surveys, honestly, but these are the basic points to be aware of.

Development administrative activities

If you are doing things right, there are always administrative tasks happening throughout the entire building cycle that are essential for your business to operate effectively and profitably. If you don't have your systems and processes established from the outset, it will be very painful to go back later to catch up.

Bookkeeping and accounting software, as I pointed out during setting up your company, for example, should be in place as soon as you start spending your very first dollar. This will make it possible to tie expenditures to specific properties, and to more easily monitor whether you're on-budget or not.

Insurance is another essential element to have in place. You'll need builder's risk insurance, meaning the coverage for the replacement of the improvements that you are building on top of the lot in the event of a loss, and liability insurance. I recommend buying liability insurance the moment that you close on the purchase of the land. Builder's risk will have to be in place by the time you close on your construction loan.

Before you break ground, all of your raw materials, labor estimates, and quotes should be in your possession, so that your budget doesn't change mid-stream and cause you to have to reassess your project. Get your prices in writing and hold onto them in your filing system or software program in the cloud.

A checklist of all the steps in your building process is part of creating a payment tracking system, together with a vendor and supplier list of all of the key contacts who are working on your project. That way you can quickly reach whoever is responsible for a particular aspect of the build.

Don't try to jump the gun and break ground until you've closed on your construction loan, because the bank will likely conduct a visual inspection prior to closing to ensure you haven't started work. Yes, a bank representative will actually drive by the land to make sure no one has touched it. That way, they can enforce their first lien, meaning that they are first in line to get their money back if anything goes wrong. If any work has been done on it, they can't exercise a first lien position. In that case, they will require details of what has been done and who did it prior to closing. You will then need to have those contractors sign affidavits that any work they did has been paid in full and receive corresponding lien releases from anyone who stepped foot on the lot.

Even as you wait for your loan closing date, you should be preparing to hit the ground running. That means getting all your ducks in a row, as they say. Meaning, you should have made all of your selections regarding interior and exterior materials and finishes; you should have it all up-to-date including current construction and development schedules; and all of your contractors and materials suppliers lined up and ready to deliver your hardware, plumbing, light fixtures, carpentry, and everything else you're going to need.

You do not want to do things as you go, or to leave too many decisions until after you break ground. Leaving decisions until later will cause delays, confusion, and increase the probability that costs will rise. Instead, you should make every possible decision before you start building. That also helps you get to know your product better, stay on budget, and confirm that the materials you need are available.

Planning up-front also helps avoid excuses from contractors who may want to claim their delay is due to not receiving selections from you about your chosen items or not having bought the materials they need. Do as much as you can up-front so that things run more smoothly once the house is under construction.

Depending on the area where you are building and the scope of work, you may be monitored by OSHA (Occupational Safety and Health Administration). They require things like helmets and facial protection, proper gear, adequate ladders, ramps and walkways, scaffolding, and a guardrail system—fall protection. OSHA wants to see a safe workplace in general and EPA (Environmental Protection Agency) requirements met for your job site, such as silt fencing to avoid discharge and construction washout, erosion and sediment control, stable soil, pollution prevention, maintaining buffers around surfaces, tree perimeter protection, and others.

Another important step before you break ground is to install temporary security fencing to protect your work area. It is very common for equipment and materials to go missing or get stolen overnight from houses that are unoccupied, so setting up a fence and security cameras help deter would-be criminals and save you some serious money.

Before you get into the actual construction process, it is useful to know how long each step of the construction process will take, so you can plan accordingly. How long does it take to frame a house, run the plumbing, electrical, or air conditioning, for example? How long does it take to get an inspection, approve, and then install a water meter in your

LAND DEVELOPMENT, CONSTRUCTION PROCESS, AND MANAGEMENT

area? These timelines are helpful so that you can build them into your own plans and ensure you finish your project as efficiently as possible.

Contractors don't schedule themselves, which can result in missing their own appointments and commitments quite often, which then affects you. This is why project managers and superintendents exist—to ensure quality and manage their schedule. Which is why it is your responsibility to create your own program of activities and to enforce them.

Find out when some of the city-related items (which are out of your control) are scheduled to happen, so you can work your other items around those dates. Don't assume your contractors are going to magically show up once the property is ready for their specific stage of the work. You will need to be proactive, expeditious, persistent, and organized, which is part of the trick in this industry.

Of course, different builders do certain things in different orders, and that's okay. Choose your style and your sequence. For example, some pour streets and driveways first to provide better and easier access to their lots, while others wait until the end to avoid damage to the concrete made by heavy equipment and delivery trucks. Whereas some start with a perimeter wood fence and then do all the undergrounds and foundations first.

> By the time you're ready to break ground, you should have all of your bids gathered, your budget finalized, and your loan closed. You should also have a full set of plans with permits as well as final renderings. Your home specifications and your selections must all be lined up, too. Making changes on paper, before construction begins, is much easier and less expensive than modifying the plan mid-project.
>
> Believe it or not, many builders break ground and *then* produce specifications and selections as they go. That's dangerous and can cause you to lose control of budgets and schedules.

Going vertical

Finally! This is the moment you've been working toward for months—the day construction of your house begins. Many builders think of this as the fun part because it's the stage at which you begin to see your vision take shape. All of the legwork that you've completed up to this point will come together. From this point on, progress will feel more tangible and be more visible than before.

Perhaps it took more time, steps, and preparations than what you had anticipated, which was not necessarily that much fun. These behind-the-scenes tasks aren't as exciting, which may be why you don't hear many people talking about it as often or why there aren't frequent episodes on your favorite interior design TV shows devoted to administrative work.

You might be surprised to know how frequently builders break ground without finalizing key decisions regarding everything from window style to finishes or appliances. They think it's an easy thing and there is no need to worry about it right now. The problem is that you will become reactive rather than proactive during the process and rushing at the last minute can overwhelm you.

The most common result is that you quickly fall behind schedule, nothing gets finished on time, and you overspend. So, kick off this next cycle of building being organized and with the vast majority of your decisions already made.

I should repeat that the earlier the stage of construction, the more critical it is, or the less possible it is to fix later on. It's not as big of a deal, relatively, to mess up a backsplash in a kitchen and have to tear it out and replace it. Or tear out carpeting, move a light fixture, or replace a door. These are finishing tasks that can be frustrating, but not especially detrimental to the overall project.

What you don't want to do is to make mistakes installing your underground plumbing, pouring the foundation in the wrong place, or trying to adjust the structure of the house once it's built. Because once it's done, there's no turning back. These early steps must be carefully monitored and completed exactly according to the plans you've designed, submitted, and had approved or you may go broke correcting mistakes. There is little margin for error with respect to these early stages, which are highly technical.

Due to the non-technical purpose of this book, I will not dive into the individual construction steps and/or details. I must assume that this portion of the business will be learned elsewhere. I will say that one of the main reasons building homes is challenging has to do with the fact that the process is happening in a very uncontrolled and inconsistent environment. You are essentially manufacturing a complex product in what is basically a moving factory, where a couple dozen different trades with different ownership, sets of skills, individual work ethics, varying management systems, strategies, philosophies, personalities, and levels of quality control will all participate. The work of one affects the work of the others and everyone's work affects your end results. Needless to say, once you get started on building,

Related to pouring concrete, builders often neglect to test the quality of the concrete that they use. Your engineering plans call for a certain density or pressure per-square-inch (PSI) specific to the design of your home. In order to comply with the required strength, you need to be sure that the cement being delivered to your construction site meets the specifications. If it doesn't, there will be potential lack of performance, such as cracks beyond acceptable parameters later on and even structural failure, which leads to lawsuits.

A simple way to prevent this is to let your contractors know that you're sampling the concrete and will have it tested. Hire a specialized lab who will take random samples confirming the correct PSI. You may not need to do this on every job, especially when you start doing significant volume, but on random houses and certainly in your high-priced homes. You don't want to discover that your contractor diluted your concrete, or they gave you less than what you paid for density-wise. But if you've warned them that you'll be testing, they are more likely to be careful.

there will be a series of points at which local inspectors need to come in and ensure that the work is being completed as per code. The number and types of inspections depend on each town, region of the country, local code, and characteristics of building and terrain, but here are the typical stages in the order they generally occur:

> Forms inspection, plumbing undergrounds, excavation, foundation, windstorm, sheathing/nail pattern plywood, roofing, siding, plumbing rough-in, A/C rough-in, electrical rough-in, framing, insulation, sheetrock, plumbing shower/tubs, plumbing top-out, final electrical, final A/C, and final home inspection.

While these are typical points at which you should expect inspections from city or town officials, you may also want to schedule your own private inspection. You will have a good twenty-five or so contractors working on your project during the process and chances are good some will make small mistakes. The local government's inspectors are checking that you've completed work that meets the local codes, or regulations, or you will get a red tag that demands you stop work until the deficiency is corrected. If it is up to code, you will get a green tag.

However, being up to code does not necessarily mean that the work is up to your high standards. Which is why you may want your own supervision or inspector to check for quality. A private inspector can check how the work is being done and whether they consider it quality craftsmanship. Your contractors are hard workers, but they may not be as focused on the smaller details as you would be. Having a third-party inspector come in to effectively rate their work can help you identify potential problem areas and raise your expectations. Especially on higher-end homes, this can be helpful.

Mistakes happen in every industry all the time and here it's no different, from technical ones to installing the wrong tile, paint color, or faucets. For that reason, you need to have someone verify the work. This is when your interior designer, if you have one, and your superintendent come in handy.

Earning cooperation from your team

Over time, you will likely work with dozens of different tradespeople and contractors. Some you may partner with once and others may become ongoing, long-term alliances. Part of the success or failure of those relationships is out of your control, but you should start to build a name for yourself now. And you want your reputation to be of someone who does what they say they will.

Just about anyone can start a business, but to become and remain successful, you need to be true to your word. This industry is full of clowns and charlatans who come and go and are known for trying to cheat people, save a buck, and cut corners whenever possible. Don't let cutbacks and slow pay be what you're known for.

Surrounding yourself with a hardworking team of employees and contractors will make it much easier for you to establish yourself as a quality home builder. It's much easier to attract like-minded people if you are a kind and respectful person. Those around you will be much more willing to support you, to work with you, if you are fair and ethical.

The majority of the individuals and companies that will work for you will be small businesses. Many take pride in the specialized work that they do and they want you to take notice of the skill that they show. They want respect. They want to be treated as fellow business owners, not employees. They want to be recognized as your colleagues and partners in the work that you're doing together, rather than underlings or employees. Because they're not. And you are dependent on their good work. They can make or break you.

To get people to do what you ask, with pleasure, you need to build camaraderie and teamwork. Because if they enjoy working for you, they will go the extra mile to make sure you and your buyer are pleased. That does not mean overlooking problems or letting little things slide that are actually unacceptable. You can enforce expectations and boundaries, as long as you do it with respect and not arrogance.

And if that doesn't work with some contractors, then try a different one on your next project. Evaluate the members of your team in category and adjust. Maybe the painter was terrific but the A/C guy was not, or the cabinet maker was amazing and the flooring guy was just awful. So don't hire the bad ones again. That's the good news about contractors—if they don't meet your expectations for quality, you can try out new ones next time.

And on the flipside, if they don't like you, if they don't respect you, if you don't have a good name, you will have a harder time keeping contractors. You will have a hard time with them showing up and making your work a priority. It's not about paying them more either. Establishing solid, respectful relationships with skilled contractors is an inexpensive way to build partnerships that will save you headaches and money in the long run.

Treat them well and get along. Do special things for them once in a while to recognize how hard they're working for you. Socialize with them now and again. Learn their names. Learn a little about them. This helps forge relationships. Every month or so at Tricon, we would barbecue up a big lunch at one of our job sites and invite all of our contractors to stop by. I can't tell you how much this helped create a culture of appreciation.

You can also build loyalty by offering ongoing work. Regular projects are preferred to higher-paying occasional jobs. Contractors want consistent work more than they want a few more dollars per job. So, the more that you can offer a steady stream of business, the more loyalty you'll build.

You are also more likely to become a favorite client if you can find a way to pay your subcontractors more frequently. Most small builders are only able to pay contractors once a job is completed, or after they get a draw from the bank. This ends up being in two or three stages. That makes it hard for subcontractors to budget, so at Tricon, we paid weekly, breaking their contracts into more progress payments. Yes, that was more recordkeeping and administrative work for us but it's much more convenient for contractors to get a little bit of weekly cash flow to cover staff and expenses than to wait until you finish the job. Since many contractors survive paycheck to paycheck, finding other ways to pay them than in lump sums at the end can earn their gratitude and loyalty, too.

When to hire your first employee

At the beginning, it's most likely that you will be your company's only employee. Being the only employee allows you, as the owner or partner, to learn every aspect of the business as well as to conserve cash. Preserving resources in your early years makes it possible to survive and later to grow faster, because you have more funds to invest in growth.

However, you will reach a point at which you simply can't do everything yourself. There are only so many hours in the day to deal with inspectors, subcontractors, brokers, banks, architects, engineers, and designers, on top of picking up necessary materials, returning emails, or catching up on paperwork. And you also need to sleep every few days, too.

Once you get to that point, or maybe even a little past it, there are two things to consider as you figure out what skills you want your first employee to have. One approach is to consider what types of tasks are taking you the most time, or which are the most distracting that you could also train someone else to do. Figure out what is eating up the biggest part of your day or your week. That's one approach.

The other thing to consider are the activities you really dislike. In fact, you dislike them so much that you may tend to put them off, or to avoid them altogether and make you dread going to work. What are the activities that are taking up a lot of your time *and* which you don't enjoy? The intersection of those two things are the skills your first employee should have, ideally.

Frequently those tasks involve one of the two extremes, being a superintendent at the job site or an office administrator/bookkeeper.

Those two types of roles tend to be the most common first hire, because those types of tasks eat up so much of your day.

Before you hand off certain tasks to someone else, however, I would definitely recommend that you do their job, or that you have done their job. Only by being familiar with their assigned tasks can you gauge how well your new employee is performing after they take it over. You'll have a better sense of how much they should be able to do in a typical day and how long tasks should take if you know how long the same tasks take you. After hiring someone else to take care of them, you can then factor in the cost of that new hire into your overhead expenses going forward.

Another duty for you to tackle as your business grows is documenting how you want things done. This is often done by drafting manuals of operation.

Creating manuals of operation

If you paid any attention to the "processes, guidelines, and procedures" section, you probably remember that you should be documenting as many of your trials and errors, victories and defeats as you identify them. As soon as you begin to see patterns for how things need to get done, take note immediately. From design procedures, accounting rules, or construction steps you want your workers to follow to increase the odds that you achieve the quality and consistency level you're after.

Not only should you write down how you want different tasks handled, but also make note of who should be doing it. Being precise with what each position is in charge of is the perfect way to build accountability for your team. If you're unclear, so will they be with results, and everyone will "pass the buck" to one another while nothing ever gets done. What is their job description? Describing the tasks they are required to complete and in what order also helps provide direction to the person who is responsible for completing each task. You are making it clear what you expect from them as far as process, timeline, and deliverable.

One of the biggest mistakes I see employers make when they hire a new employee is that they are not specific about what they want and expect from that individual. They are left to flounder as they try to figure out how to best do their job. Don't leave that up to chance. Instead, instruct them regarding exactly what you want them to do, step by step. If anything is vague, you run the risk of the employee completing the task incorrectly and then blaming you for the lack of specificity. Everyone in your organization needs to be clear about what their job entails, how it supports the overall functioning of the business, and on what metrics they will be evaluated.

Your job descriptions and roles will certainly evolve over time, too, especially as your business grows. For example, when you're starting out and you're building one or maybe two houses, you don't need a dedicated warranty person or a purchasing department. There just isn't enough work to justify paying someone to do only warranty or purchasing-related tasks. However, once you're building dozens of homes, your superintendent, for example, doesn't have time to go meet with every buyer about warranties. At that point, you need to restructure the way things are done and determine who does what. But the business will dictate at what point you'll need to start adding those departments;

Avoid the trap that many entrepreneurs fall into when they hire their first employee. What some new business owners do is hire someone to be their shadow, essentially—to follow them around and learn the business so that they can eventually take over what you, the owner, do. Unfortunately, this job description is too general and the new hire ends up doing next to nothing, because they have no specific responsibilities. Instead, hire someone to take over one area of your business that you are weak at. They can certainly expand their role over time to take on more responsibility, but it is better at the start to assign specific tasks than to hope your new hire identifies a function where they are of most use.

---

you just need to pay attention and be proactive. That will most likely happen naturally, when you're working on projections within your business and you're looking ahead to the next year or two's volume of business.

It's always better to identify in advance the point at which your schedule is going to be overbooked, so that you can start planning accordingly to bring someone new on and still have time to train them. If you wait to hire someone until you don't have time to sleep, you're so busy, you may rush their training, which could hurt your productivity and effectiveness overall. So, make that decision to add another employee when you see that you have multiple houses in the works but before you are completely overwhelmed and trying to juggle too much.

It will also be less stressful financially because you should be able to see in your revenue projections that the business can support an additional salary. And to reduce your chances of picking the wrong person, which is not so unusual, remember to be thorough while interviewing and making your selection. Don't get completely discouraged if the first person you hired didn't meet your expectations and you end up going back to square one looking for a replacement. It happens to all of us.

CHAPTER 8

Financial Management and Market Conditions

At the core of humanity's progress, innovation and success are the frequent and reoccurring discussions about how to raise and manage money. After all, this is a big part of the essence of capitalism and also the soul of this book. So, don't be surprised if I keep hammering you with it. Unfortunately, whether you're an incredible artist, a talented bohemian, or a highly technical inventor, your gift—your skills and your craft—cannot be exposed to the world or even have a chance to survive unless you educate yourself in the world of cold hard cash.

When you're managing a multifaceted business consisting of many subcontractors, suppliers, customers, employees, and invoices with partial billing, it is easy to lose track of your money. Not only do you need to stay on top of how much is going out, but you should also closely monitor what's coming in and whether it's sufficient to cover your cash requirements. That way you won't ever come up short. Being unable to pay bills in a timely manner can quickly damage your business' performance and reputation. It can also cause your work in progress to come to a halt.

As your company grows, expenses can sneak up on you and accumulate more quickly than you anticipate. You don't want to be caught off guard and without cash. To avoid that, you should create systems to track your finances.

Managing cash and tracking finances

It's important to be aware of your business's increasing monetary demands, which may not be directly related to the physical progress on the house(s) you're building. As I previously explained, expenses related to the building process are referred to as "vertical," but there are also those other categories to consider, which can quickly get out of hand if you aren't watching them like a hawk.

That is why I created tools to make monitoring my business simpler and easier, and so should you. Through the years I've used numerous checklists, document lists, spreadsheets, visuals, copies of bids and sample purchase orders, a pro forma, a budget, timeline, and schedule, among other tools. However, my cash report is the one I refer to daily. It doesn't need to be overly sophisticated, but it must look several weeks and even months ahead, allowing you to visualize what your financial needs will be.

My cash report gives me a comprehensive view of where my money is, from what's currently scheduled to come in, what's going out, and when, which I consider to be one of my most important tools. Shortages can always occur, especially as you grow, regardless of the pace at which the business expands. However, the expenses that can take you off course are more likely to be unrelated to the actual building of the house. This becomes a larger issue the more homes you're building simultaneously.

When you go from one project to two, then four, then eight or sixteen, small collateral expenses start piling up. As your project count grows, so does your number of employees, the software fees you use to manage the business, the property taxes, and your carrying costs on multiple houses. With several houses, you have ongoing cleaning and contingency costs, advances, insurance, administrative expenses, office supplies, rent, and so on. Before you know it, those expenses have grown larger than you might have expected. It is also common to begin tying up properties for future developments while you are still working on current ones. Which means you're likely to be spending money on preliminary "soft" phases of those potential sites before you've even secured a new investment to cover them. It is very normal to use cash from your operations thinking that it will not cause much impact, because the amounts are small, but they add up. Before you know it, you have no idea what went where and why you're short!

For that reason, you'll want to begin separating accounts by house and by development, "current and upcoming," to help you more accurately tally how much cash will be going out every month for every single category. Unless you keep expenses separate, it is also difficult to distinguish profitable houses from the failed ones; they can all end up blending together. As you start planning to reproduce similar developments, you can see the results of your current ones to help you make better decisions.

Cash flow is not just a game of money, it's also a game of timing. The key to cash management is not only to have the amount you need, but most importantly to have it by the time you need it. Not having the right amount of cash at the right time is the leading cause for bankruptcy! Although I review my cash report daily, you don't have to do so as frequently. However, I would recommend looking at it at least weekly, and to spend enough time carefully brainstorming and forecasting the financial activity that will be happening. This way, you can see how much you need for each of the major categories, as well as planning how to cover them with the funds that you project coming in.

Coming in:

- Construction draws
- Investor equity
- Investor loans
- Home sales
- Others

Going out:

- Overhead and payroll
- Construction vendors and contractors
- Land development vendors and contractors
- Bank interest payments
- Investor distributions
- Deposits
- Advances
- Land acquisitions
- Equity requirements
- Property taxes
- Credit card payments
- Others

The point is to always ensure that you have more money coming in than going out. If you aren't looking far enough ahead at the funds that your business will require to remain functioning, you could suddenly realize that you're in trouble at the last minute and not have enough time to do something about it.

You need to be looking ahead at how many houses you're starting and what the associated needs and monthly expenses will be for each. A cash projection is looking ahead, to anticipate and be able to act in plenty of time to secure a loan or find an investor if you identify the shortage.

The thing about cash management is that it can be deceiving. There are times where you may have excess capital in your account and decide to spend it on something that's not a priority, then when an urgent need comes up, you realize the bad choices you made. I've been there many times. If you can look ahead and see that you could be out of cash in week four, you can take steps to avoid that. For example, you could delay the start of a project that requires up-front deposits, pick up the pace on another property to be able to collect a draw on it, or extend and put off purchasing another property in order to hold on to the cash longer. It's all about timing.

I should point out that over the years, I've often encountered new entrepreneurs that confuse the meaning of cash flow, assets, and profits. Although they all appear to be similar, these three terms are completely different subjects. *Cash flow* refers to money flowing in that is available to you now or will be in the short-term. What's confusing is that cash flow could either be an asset if it's coming from revenues related to the sale of a house, or a liability if it's coming from borrowed money via a bank draw or an investor loan that must be paid back. The important part is that cash flow is simply money at your disposal that can solve your immediate problems. *Assets* are all the things of value that your company owns both liquid and non-liquid, and *profits* refer to the net difference between the total cost of your finished products and the amount that you sell them for. Although all assets have value, they may not all be liquid and if they are tied up in land, equipment, or other existing projects when you need cash, they won't get you out of trouble. The key word is "availability" of those resources.

Pros and cons of leverage

Growing is always difficult in such a capital-intensive industry. In order to obtain one single additional customer, you must invest a very large amount of money and time before you see any benefits. Normally, if you wait until you develop, build, complete, sell, close, and fund one of your projects before securing your next one, you may realize that by that time your living expenses for the duration of the project either matched or even exceeded the profits, bringing you right back to square one. Leverage is the way to multiply your production, but that means debt. Like most veteran entrepreneurs who have been through many economic cycles, I have a love-hate relationship with leverage, or taking on debt to fund business growth. Leverage can act like steroids for business, making it possible to grow much faster than without external capital and exponentially increase profits. But since leverage involves borrowing money from banks or financial institutions, there is risk involved.

You need access to cheap money to grow any business, which a bank can provide. If you have collateral and can put up some equity, banks can lend to you less expensively than other alternatives. That's the advantage of leverage—that it can be less expensive than your other financing options. When times are good, leverage can help you buy many properties with minimum equity—effectively spreading out your money over a greater number of projects. This can turbocharge growth.

On the flip side, however, is the disadvantage, or con, which is that if you encounter any bumps in the road and you're unable to make your monthly payments on time, the bank can step in and take ownership of your properties. Like everything else, there's always a catch. That inexpensive cash comes with a lot of monitoring, rules, regulations, and conditions that are not flexible. If you don't follow them, you can lose it all—quickly.

Investors, who are another option, are more like business partners. Unlike banks, which cost less but also hold a first lien position on your project, investors' money is only repaid after the bank. That creates a greater risk for investors and for that risk they want a greater return. Depending on different factors, including the developer's credentials and track record, investors can take an equity position in the project of twenty percent, thirty percent, and even more of the profits. By taking an ownership stake, they will own part of the proceeds, but they're in it with you. If you win, they win, and if you fail, they fail. So, they're going to do what they can to support you and be more patient, so that everybody wins. Because their goals are aligned with yours, they may be willing to wait for their payout on the backend when profit can be maximized. Investors generally understand that the market is fluid and that forcing a sale right this moment, in order to get their money back, may not make both of you the most money.

Where the bank has terms, restrictions, covenants, contracts, deadlines, and limitations that dictate exactly what you'll pay and when, investors focus more on maximizing the return on their investment, even if they have to wait a little longer to get it. Banks also have to deal with government regulators and examiners limiting them from any change of plans, so even if they wanted to help, their hands are tied.

When leverage makes sense

Despite the extra guardrails banks put in place when they lend you money to ensure you'll pay it back, under the right circumstances, borrowing from banks can work well. I liken leverage to steroids because, like steroids, if you get an injury, a steroid shot can provide immediate relief from your pain. And if you abuse it, it can take you down. If you ignore your bank's requirements and repayment demands, there will be repercussions. They will take ownership of your home. The same goes when you borrow too much.

What's important to understand about leverage is timing. If your timing is good, leverage can make you rich. That extra money you've borrowed can work as a catapult to move you forward. It can help you grow quicker and cheaper. But in a bad economy, leverage becomes dead weight that can drown you.

Here's how that can happen. Let's say you borrow $1 million from the bank at seven percent, or at whatever the current rate is. In exchange for lending you the money, the bank requires that you make payments monthly. That's mandatory, no matter what's going on in the market or with your business. For example, let's say that for whatever reason your development takes longer to build. Your house isn't completed as soon as you expected and you start running out of time to sell the property and can no longer make those interest payments; the bank can't do anything about it. It expects its monthly check. There are very few repayment options. And if you don't pay on time, they will tack on interest and fees and eventually take possession of the house. The interest banks charge is lower than investors, but they are risk-averse, which means they expect you to come forward with results.

On the other hand, if you explain your situation to your investor, they may be much more flexible regarding repayment terms. They want their money, of course, but they are willing to take a bigger risk on the project than the bank is. And, obviously, they want a bigger return for that risk-taking.

A situation that almost forced my brother and I out of business during the financial crisis and housing bubble of 2008 was borrowing for land, which is something I highly discourage you from doing. Allow me to explain. When you borrow money to build a house, you have essentially secured your financial ability to complete a consumer product that can be taken to market. If the tide turns, builders can easily discount the house to sell faster. By reducing the sales price, you can be assured of at least getting the original investment out in the end. Even if the market takes a dive, you should still be able to sell the house at your cost, pay everyone, and move on.

Here's what I mean. Let's say that the total cost of your home was $450,000 and you had planned to sell it for $525,000, including your profit. If the economy crashes, normally there are investors willing to buy a house under market value if you're willing to drop your price. That means that if you can stomach selling it at your total cost of $450,000, you will have lost time but not money, and this will allow you to avoid bankruptcy and live to see another day.

That $75,000 difference between your cost and your projected sales price is the cushion that I am referring to.

When it comes to land, on the other hand, you don't have that cushion because you bought it for what it costs, without having yet added any value to it. When the economy crashes, nobody in their right mind wants to buy anything at market value. Also with land, the pool of buyers is much, much smaller. Instead of being a very broad audience, land buyers are reduced to builders and developers. When you decide you need to fire-sale a house, you have many prospects looking to move into the neighborhood at a discounted price. However, when you decide to drop the price on a piece of land, your only buyers are other builders. And when the market goes bad, builders are not looking for more land to buy.

Which is how I almost went broke when I had close to $40 million in land loans. I had to hold onto the land because I couldn't find a buyer, but to maintain ownership I had to find a way to make the loan payments or I'd lose the millions of dollars I originally invested.

Since I couldn't interest any builders in buying our land, even for the amount that we owed the bank, and I didn't want to effectively go bankrupt overnight, I chose to build my way out. Let me rephrase that, I was *forced* to build my way out. I continued making loan payments with the few dollars that came in, using all sales proceeds including our original equity, basically putting back money that we had already made in previous years. That was painful. I actually didn't have much of a choice. Here's why. Let's say that for every $1 million of land that we owned, $700,000 was owed to the bank. The market got to where I couldn't even sell it for that loan amount. Selling would mean that, for starters, we would lose $300,000 of our equity for every $1 million of land, plus having to bring additional money to closing to make up the difference, which we didn't have. We would be basically subsidizing our land to the next buyer in the form of a margin. To avoid bankruptcy, we kept operating one day at a time, supporting all of our overhead plus those $40+ million in land loans alone. That was one of the toughest times of my business career. I didn't sleep well for a few years, but somehow, we survived.

The financial world is an interesting one, because depending on your perspective, we were either completely broke or still multi-millionaires, which is what I mean about the importance of cash flow. On paper we had close to $100 million in non-liquid assets and as long as we did not get rid of those upside-down properties, therefore "realizing" our losses, we were still rich. But in the real world, at that particular time, the market was not willing to give the same value to those assets. As long as I was able to keep up with those payments, we were still very bankable. We were just extremely tight on cash and needed to figure out how to gain time while the market came back. Being able to weather the storm, of course, was easier said than done.

During the downturn, banks not only wanted interest payments punctually but, to make matters worse, once many of those loans matured, some banks wanted to be paid back in full. They were not willing to renew the loans—they wanted out. This was a horrible period that caught many of us off guard. Surviving became a full-time job.

We had to figure out not just how to pay interest, property taxes, payroll, and overhead, but also where to come up with cash or with new lines of credit to pay existing loans that were not being renewed. I can honestly say that I got a PhD in high-stakes negotiations and in shuffling millions of dollars back and forth each day. When we finally had enough money to continue building, we did so through the few banks willing to convert those land loans into construction loans. One house at a time, we worked for a few years to pay every obligation and avoid bankruptcy, but at the price of gradually diluting our equity and losing millions of our already earned profits.

Those were scary years, but they also earned me a lot of credibility in the industry as I made everyone whole at the expense of giving back most of the wealth that my brother and I had accumulated. I am most proud to say that through the catastrophe that literally went on for years, my brother and I never once had a single argument, regardless of how many millions we were losing right and left. That's what a true partnership is. Had we not had land loans and only home construction loans, the impact would have been much less, which is why I'm recommending that you *not* take out loans to buy land. The lesson is that leverage works as long as you maintain cash reserves to service the debt for the duration of the project.

Removing emotion from the process

Homebuilding is a long and very tough process, so it's important to remove emotion as much as possible from business decisions. You need to become logical and pragmatic. It is very easy to treat business choices as personal ones, and to get emotionally connected to your product, much like investors get carried away when watching the stock market. You can't let your heart rule your head or you will likely put yourself in a vulnerable position in this business.

Although it's difficult to separate yourself from a project you've worked so long and hard on, you need to avoid falling in love with the houses you build. Don't let your pride and ego get in the way of running your company, because it becomes more difficult to think clearly when making important financial decisions.

A house is a product. Yes, you had a lot to do with the way it turned out, and it is now a reflection of who you are as a builder, so it's normal to feel like it's your baby. You also devoted a year or two of your life to finding the land, developing it, getting all the permits, risking your savings, getting in debt, building it, suffering through plenty of stress, plus 1,000 headaches, only to face the possibility of losing money on it. That's the reality. Not every property will be a big win. But if you begin making decisions based on what you personally want or expect, you may end up in trouble. Keep the integrity of your company as your first priority, as opposed to focusing on the specific results of any one project.

Emotion is especially dangerous when it comes to pricing or convincing yourself that your house is flawless in every possible way. You may have a number you're hoping to get for the house you built, but the reality is that the market will dictate what is fair and appropriate—not you. You may believe that the home is worth at least $650,000, based on what you invested and all the work you put in, but what home buyers are willing to pay at the moment you market it is what will set the price. The market is bigger than all of us and it will determine the price on its own. Fortunately, the market will also talk back to you, to let you know how close you are to the true price: through traffic, feedback from buyers, and offers.

If you have a lot of traffic coming through the house, chances are good that there is a buyer in that pool of visitors. Of course, the more traffic, the better your odds. It becomes a numbers game and you only need one serious buyer to win. But if you have no traffic, that means the house is either overpriced or you have the wrong product for the market you're in. You can fix both of those things, to a certain extent, fortunately. You can drop your price, which I know you don't want to do, and you can listen to the feedback you're getting from people who tour the house. What are their objections? Can you easily address them? If you hear feedback that the colors are wrong or the cabinets are bad, the simple response to the agent is that you'd be happy to change them if they include the request in their offer.

Granted, there are some things that are just not fixable. You can't make a small yard bigger, add more closets, or change the room dimensions, for example. But if you're hearing that the rooms are too small, you can certainly stage them with smaller pieces of furniture and/or add lighting to make them feel larger.

If you're getting a lot of traffic and no offers, you may have the wrong agent. Typically, within the first thirty days you'll gather enough feedback to let you know what people like and don't like about the property. You have a chance then to address what you can in order to increase the odds of going under contract. You want an offer sooner rather than later, of course, because each additional day you own that property, the more money it's costing you.

Which is yet another reason to remove all emotion from the process of selling the house you've just built. It's not *your* home. You're not going to live in it. What you need is to find a buyer willing to pay you more than you spent building it, so that you can move on and build your next house. And you want to do that quickly, to reduce your accumulated costs. I am not suggesting that you should leave money on the table by giving in right away to the first person who walks in. You should certainly negotiate aggressively, but at the end of the day, do whatever you can to avoid letting buyers walk away. I call it stretching the rubber band as much as possible without breaking it. Each month you continue to own a house, the more your carrying costs increase while the value of the property declines. If the market takes a turn for the worse, it generally stays that way for a while.

Also, don't expect to make a lot of money on every deal. If you do, that's wonderful, but it's unlikely you'll hit it out of the park every time. However, you can still work to build a positive reputation no matter what, and there is value in that. There is still some benefit in successfully delivering a home even without the anticipated profit. When you complete and sell a home, no one else will know whether you made money or not, but they will see that you finished it and sold it, which helps you establish a history, a track record, and credibility in the market that can help you start and sell your next property. It builds your résumé, which contributes to your personal growth and improves your chances of continued success.

Minimizing your investment risk

How you use your money can help minimize your investment risk. There is no one right answer or approach here, however. You can opt to invest more in a property and earn less percentage of a return because it's a safer asset, or you can take a bigger risk in pursuit of greater reward.

Let me give you some examples of some potential choices. Let's say one option is to buy a $500,000 lot. You can split it into two properties and build two houses. Your projections suggest that you can sell each home for $600,000 and make a profit of ten percent, or $60,000 per house, for a total of $120,000. That equates to a twenty-four percent cash-on-cash return. Or you can go to a more speculative neighborhood in transition and buy the same $500,000 lot, on which you can put ten houses selling them for $300,000 each. Each of the houses are projected to generate the same ten percent profit of $30,000. That is a $300,000 total profit, providing a sixty percent cash-on-cash return.

So, the question is, do you invest $500,000 to make $120,000 by building two homes in a traditional neighborhood? Or do you invest that same amount to make $300,000—nearly three times as much and in a less proven, transitional area?

Keep in mind that for a number of reasons, sales in transitional neighborhoods tend to slow down sooner when the general economy retreats. That's because buyers in those neighborhoods, in addition to wanting to upgrade from an apartment to a new home with more space and luxury, also see an opportunity to profit from buying early in the revitalization and beautification process of a neighborhood. The neighborhood may not actually be their first choice. They're likely not upgrading from another home; they may be trying to move out of an apartment, but if they can't raise enough money for the down payment, they'll have to wait.

Normally in a neighborhood where buyers have more disposable income, more liquid assets, they may be less impacted immediately by an economic downturn. They buy simply because they want to be there, and they can afford it. It is typically easier to sell homes in established neighborhoods, but your potential return could be lower because the neighborhood is already expensive and pretty. There is less upside appreciation potential than in an up-and-coming area. Meaning: lower risk.

If you picture a graph illustrating "buying as a necessity and as an opportunity" rather than "buying what you want where you want," the number of buyers moves lower (i.e., fewer of them) as the price point gets higher. Of course, there is a lot more to this, as there are many other economic components to consider. You never know what sector of the market will slow down more, or when, because the issues that impact lower price points are different from the ones affecting pricier homes. For example, a credit crunch, inflation, higher interests, or high unemployment may affect the lower price points more, as the rich are not so worried about that. On the other hand, an election year, a stock market crash, or a war overseas causing uncertainty may impact the higher price points, where lower income families may not be remotely concerned about those issues during their buying process. This is certainly a long and complicated subject, but the point is that there are always buyers waiting to live in the nicer neighborhoods for the right price. On the other hand, at every price bracket increase, the pyramid of buyers gets exponentially smaller. The pricier the home, the fewer the people who can afford it, so this is a long discussion for another time.

You can manage your risk by being clear about how much money you are comfortable having tied up in one project. If you're comfortable taking on the obligation to build ten homes, then the riskier proposition may be the best choice *for you*.

You can also reduce your risk by understanding the market you're building in, by becoming more familiar with it, by reworking your financial projections until you perfect them, and by questioning your true comfort level with risk. Look at the available inventory in those areas, too, because if there is limited inventory in one area, there may be more opportunity there simply *because* there is so little available. Being able to recognize signs regarding where the market is headed, is critical for making informed decisions regarding your own risk tolerance. If the market is on an upswing, both of those examples could be equally appealing to you if you're confident you'll be able to sell anything you build. But if the market is sketchy or the pace of home sales seems to be slowing, you might make a different decision.

All markets have their own risks. For example, lower price points may have tighter margins. Then again, higher price points require more capital, so, ultimately, your decision regarding these two options may come down to which you prefer. You may enjoy ultra-high-end finishes, so fewer homes could be better. But if you're excited by the opportunity to jump into building ten homes with a big upside because your objective is volume, then that may be the best choice for you. Or maybe your gut will tense up when you consider having to build and sell ten homes in order to get your money back. The last thing you want to do is to regret your choice, so follow your vision and your instincts.

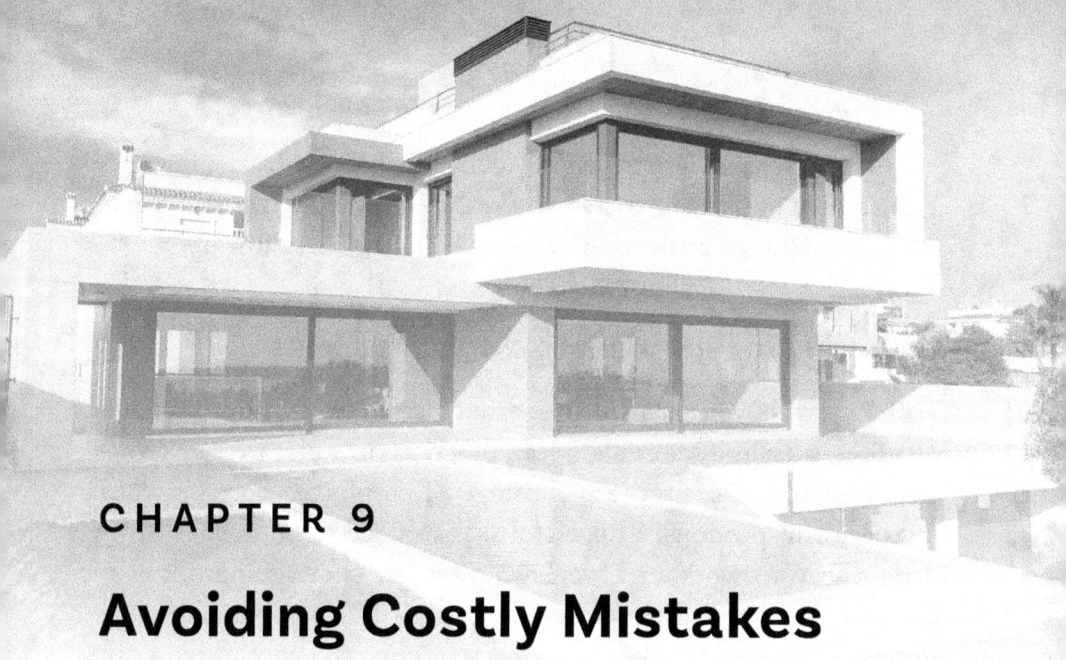

CHAPTER 9

Avoiding Costly Mistakes

As I keep repeating, no matter how much you plan, how carefully you estimate and budget, and how critical you are with hiring contractors, there will always be surprises in the home building process. That's a given.

You will come across problems you missed in the plans, or inspections and situations will arise that you could not have anticipated. The long list of potential scenarios you could face, of course, always starts with going over budget. But the list also includes things like delays with deliveries, random mistakes, contractors not showing up or even walking away altogether, lost items, theft, leaks, broken items, bad weather, accidents, red tags, changes in code, interpretations of code, bad craftmanship, materials on backorder, inventory issues, human errors, underground surprises, inspectors with different opinions, items that made sense on paper but not as much at the site, selections that looked great in a presentation package but not so much once installed, a lot of "he said/she said" throughout the entire process, and the list goes on...

Although there are preventive steps I'll share with you, I'm also going to try to prepare you so you can minimize the list and avoid getting caught off guard when challenges and crises show up.

Preparing for surprises and contingencies

To be clear, however, there is a difference between unpredictable surprises, such as a water main leak that cuts off water to your property temporarily, a city-wide shortage of employees delaying your utilities or inspections, a huge storm that came through your town damaging your work, or a worldwide lumber shortage putting you on hold, and then there are contingencies that you should actually plan for because they are relatively common in the industry. Contingencies require you to spend money you've set aside for them and include situations you should attempt to anticipate, such as an air-conditioning unit or water heater getting stolen, making repairs, or your roofing contractor falling behind and slowing your progress. For these, there's always a line item in your budget but that you hope you never have to use.

Although these two types of situations have the same end result—higher costs and potential delays—they are slightly different because some of them have a better chance of being prevented than others. Here's how:

Surprises

Home building is essentially a manufacturing process. Granted, it's moveable manufacturing, a moving factory, but home construction does have a standard process, just like a manufacturing line. There is a standard sequence of events, but beyond that, there is little in the way of consistency.

Even though you are one builder, one company, and one brand producing every one of your homes, each is manufactured in a different location. This is in contrast to the typical manufacturing process where materials and staff operate in one place. Essentially, you are picking up and transporting your factory each time to where the construction is occurring. You have a rotating set of players and components, from contractors to employees to workers within each crew. That ever-changing cast of characters and conditions can lead to issues regarding quality. In spite of the fact that many workers are very good at what they do, and they're by and large hard workers, in many cases they are not detail-oriented. That can create surprises when you discover that one of them ran the air-conditioning duct work differently than the other, thereby affecting how it's connected from the first to the second floor and encroaching on some closet space. Or maybe the framer installed uneven wood and inaccurate distances between the nails or between the beams. Even if you had two homes with the same floor plan, the two houses would not be identical, especially when you do low volume, because there is inconsistency built into the process; many of the instructions are left to interpretation. As a result, two crews will build two slightly different houses even when handed the exact same plans. The quality of materials is inconsistent, inspectors and their standards differ, and workers have varying levels of performance. This all leads to a series of variances within the home building process.

While one millimeter difference here or there may not be noticeable to the naked eye, those millimeters do add up, especially when not discovered immediately. Just imagine miscalculating the precise height between the first and second level of a house so that you end up with an extra half a step on the staircase. Over the course of the project, many millimeter differences can result in gaps, or overlaps. Even centimeter differences can cause issues with respect to improperly installed windows, siding, sagging floors, or cracks and waves in walls, which can cause expensive warranty issues. This is why it is so critical to have a project manager or superintendent continuously overseeing all of the work.

The importance of being present on your job site

Nowadays, micromanaging generally sounds outdated and uncomfortable, but when it comes to construction, it needs to happen. Without careful oversight you can constantly miss important details that lead to failed interim inspections of the various parts of your house. This can create a domino effect that causes your whole schedule to go off course. Which is why you or someone you trust needs to be on-site expediting and monitoring construction, to confirm everything is going as planned.

Where many manufacturing plants have in place sophisticated ISO 9001 Quality Standards, machinery, and high-tech tools designed to ensure that every output is identical, the home construction industry does not. Workers in our business are trained differently, use different tools, and still rely on basic measurement devices and manual tactics, such as counting nails per drywall sheet and using their own level or measuring tape (meaning, not very sophisticated). To most construction workers, the meaning of the word quality is subjective and extremely abstract. Their main objective is to be done, collect their money, and move on to the next job. For that reason, there is the potential for a lot of variation throughout the process that you are responsible for. Just be aware of it and watch for it.

Another related issue is the lack of any kind of operations manual that can be distributed to all of your contractors. And even if there was, no one would follow it unless you are there to enforce it. There is no one specific way to complete a task, so all of your contractors and subs are effectively working à la carte. The situation is very similar to a restaurant hiring seven different chefs to cook a different night each week. Even with a very detailed recipe for how to make, say, chicken piccata, pasta Bolognese or a Caesar salad, you are going to get seven slightly different variations on that dish. Because regardless of having that source of information, they will each use their personal touch. The same is true in home construction. With different crews, different training, and different mentalities, what you get as far as sheetrock texture, cabinet installation, or painting is going to vary. The only way to improve the consistency across your houses is to always be there, watch their work process closely, and provide ongoing feedback about how you want it done.

Speed is another potential source of inconsistency that can result in surprises because everyone rushes. Since most contractors are paid when they complete their task, the sooner it's done, the sooner they get their money. They're incentivized to hurry, so don't assume that they will meet your expectations. Help them focus and teach them to better understand your definition of quality and workmanship.

One of the frequent problems with hurrying or with carelessness is not just that work gets done incorrectly, but also that other already-completed work can be damaged. For example, you get your cabinets installed but don't protect them, so when the careless countertop supplier comes in to install your granite, they scratch up and break one of the cabinets. Then when the next guy comes in to install the doorknobs, he may place his tools on the new countertops and scratch or even break those. Later, the painter stops by to touch up the walls and leaves paint stains on your beautiful, brand-new hardwood floors—and round and round you go.

Every crew comes in to do their job and doesn't always care or pay attention to the work other crews have completed; they are intently focused on their own tasks. Every stage of the construction literally requires an entirely different company, which is only paying attention to what they are doing and not to everything else happening with your project. You will have a company come and do one thing and when they're done, they leave. Then another to perform a different task and again, they leave, and so on and so forth. Unfortunately, while they're doing their work, they may damage the work that one of the previous companies completed, which you then have to fix. One of the tricky parts is catching it when it happens, otherwise they will very likely deny it and blame someone else. Maybe the tile guy comes in to install the backsplash and a window ends up broken, but you can't prove it was the tiler, and he may not even have noticed because he was so focused on his task. He's not really worrying about what's going on around him.

As work gets done, things get broken. It can feel like two steps forward and one step back at times, unless you are there and can determine who scratched the floor or broke the tile, for example, in which case you can force them to pay for the fix. But if you're not, you now have to absorb the cost of the repair.

Some of these issues are simple to correct but other small errors can often escalate. For example, a sheetrock installer or carpenter puts a nail through the wall and perforates a pipe, so that when you turn on the water later it floods your entire house and causes extensive damage. We've experienced many examples of these minor "omissions" that went very badly, like tubs or dishwashers installed but not properly connected and when the water is turned on, it ran all over and destroyed ceilings and floors. Something as simple as a worker leaving a balcony door open or unlocked, followed by an overnight storm that floods your home, can turn into a nightmare, not to mention trying to figure out who left the door open. By being there, you minimize incidents, eliminating confusion and doubt as to who did what. That way, you can prevent or back-charge the responsible contractor for the mistake or the breakage.

These minor mishaps can also get harder to address the more they accumulate. If you don't catch them immediately, they are harder to identify and to assign blame.

Be aware that what you see on construction plans is different when you view it in 3D and in real life. The perspective looks very different on paper than it does when you're standing in the room. For that reason, you will typically need to make small adjustments here and there during the construction process, once you spot issues in the physical space. You'll be pivoting and adjusting and revising throughout the entire construction process, in order to connect what was designed on paper with what it looks like in physical form, in real life.

Ultimately, management is such a key component in construction that I would definitely prefer having the right supervisor over the right contractor. Of course, ideally, I want both, but if I had to choose, the right manager could raise the bar of every contractor that goes through the house, as opposed to having the luck to find a couple of dozen great contractors for each and every construction step. This way you could even afford to mix in a less expensive, sub-par contractor here and there when you know you'll be watching them carefully.

Documenting details and errors

During our section in chapter 4 dedicated to processes, guidelines, and procedures, I mentioned the importance of learning from our mistakes. Now let's dig deeper. The key to improving as a builder and getting errors corrected quickly and inexpensively is to pay close attention as work is being completed and to document things in real time.

In my opinion, just like with surprises and delays, there are two main categories of mistakes: 1) Someone deviated from your plans, omitted, changed, and/or damaged something and 2) the contractor did the work as designed but your idea was wrong to begin with and the design was inadequate or defective. The first type of error is fixable. Those errors are applying the wrong color paint or breaking a tile after it was installed. But the second type may not be, or at least it may not be fixable for a price that makes sense. If a closet was designed too small, or a dining room too narrow, the fix may require major restructuring, but that generally costs more money than it's worth, even if you were to have the space to do it.

The reality is that in some cases, it's not possible or feasible to make a correction. Maybe the design was off a few inches or something wasn't taken into account in the process and a flaw arises. If it can't be fixed, you can always figure out how to work around it in order to sell the home.

Consider ways to attractively cover up and distract the problem, or maybe play it up as a design feature, if you can, when you're selling the home. For example, maybe the windows ended up being lower than their ideal location or where originally planned. The benefit is that you have more sunlight coming in. And then make note of the issue with the design so that you don't repeat it on the next house. There are always things you can improve in a plan, as long as you record them so you remember them.

Liens and lien releases

This segment of the book alone can one day save you from a real nightmare. I've been through this horrible experience, which took me time to recover from. As a builder, you might think that paying your bills is the entire scope of your financial responsibility, which is already difficult enough. Unfortunately, that's not true, it's not enough. We're all familiar with the fact that if you don't pay the bank or your vendors and contractors, they can sue you and/or place a lien on your property. Recording that debt on the title of the home effectively blocks you from selling it until you pay them. But there's more to this, which is the part that not many people know about.

Many contractors and subcontractors actually do their own subcontracting but don't tell you. When you think you're hiring a specific company, they are doing some hiring of their own behind the curtain. They will often use other smaller companies to assist with a portion of their duties, like labor, buying materials, or equipment rentals, such as trucks, scaffolding, or forklifts. So, for example, when you hire a foundation company, you assume that they used their own machinery, concrete, and crews, but that may not necessarily be the case.

When the work is completed, you naïvely proceed with full payment, only to one random day receive a nasty lien notice stating that you have yet to pay for the foundation of your home(s). At that point you assume that it's all a big mistake, because you don't even know the person or company claiming to be owed money. Unfortunately, as you investigate further, you then realize that the debt is indeed real. Yes, that is correct, what you thought had been fully paid for is not, and you're now in trouble because you don't have money to pay for that same item twice. The problem is that when someone contracted by you hires or buys things delivered to your address, and for the benefit and improvement of your property, you become legally responsible for those bills, because the work was done on your house.

For example, let's say you pay a plumber for work, including all the plumbing fixtures. However, after paying the plumber you discover they didn't pay the supplier for the materials used in your house. Because the supplier wasn't paid by the plumber, they can place a lien on your property, where the work was done. Unless the plumber takes care of that bill, you're still accountable. This happens all too frequently, unfortunately. If you are lucky, when something like this happens, the contractor you hired will still be in business and has the means to make you whole. But if they have vanished or have no money to pay, you're on your own. Explaining the proceedings following this fiasco would make it a very long chapter, but you now at least know that this scenario is a real possibility. I'll leave you with the message of trying to avoid this in the first place.

One way to reduce the chances of this happening is to hire well-established companies that have a smaller chance of not paying their own bills. Also, always demand a lien release signed for the amount that you paid each contractor. It will help you if this were to ever get to court, making the contractor much more legally accountable. That will also prevent them from ever claiming that you didn't pay or that you shorted their pay. Get a release after every payment. It's not fool-proof, but it helps reduce problems down the line. My favorite and most effective preventive system is to pay for the materials portion of the job directly to the source and not to the contractor. I also like to monitor my subcontractors' accounts payables, for accounts related to my jobs, but that, of course, requires more time effort on your part. This means one more administrative duty added to your list.

Another thing that happens not too often, is that some of these so-called contractors who you think are credible, are actually just middlemen. They take your contract and go hire the actual contractor, so be careful who you hire.

Understanding the effects of accumulated delays

Delays are a normal occurrence that are also difficult to prevent. Over the years I've learned that an isolated delay here and there is not a big deal. The problem is that isolated delays occurring throughout the process don't ever happen just once. When you look back, you realize that the combined delays caused by every participant in the entire chain of events manage to accumulate into one huge delay at a scale that you never imagined. Although you'd think the concept of a delay is fairly simple—it is extra time required to complete a task beyond the originally scheduled deadline—because there are so many potential sources of delays, it can be tricky to determine the exact cause and even more complex to limit the delays to a single task. Every step can generate a delay and before you know it, you will have completely lost track of how months of progress were lost. There are, literally, a thousand things that need to happen between the time you enter into a contract to purchase a lot or property and the time you sell it. And the clock starts ticking as soon as you put down your earnest money deposit. I often say that this business is not just managing a construction site but just as important, it is managing time and money. The business does not work if any of those pieces fail.

From the moment you start doing your due diligence—you start reviewing your title work, running your numbers, getting your financing in order, preparing your plans, processing permits, ordering inspections, ordering surveys, dealing with engineers and service providers of all varieties during this first phase of work alone—it's easy to lose track of time. After that first phase you have several more, each with potential tasks that can cause delays. The more steps to be completed in your process, the more the potential delays.

Just imagine that you'll have fifty different professionals and contractors working on your house at various stages of construction and development. If each contractor gets even one day behind, you're at least fifty days behind in that timeframe. Unfortunately, the reality is that when delays occur, they usually last more than a single day. On top of that, when one contractor gets delayed, it can push back a whole series of tasks and cause even longer delays, because multiple contractors have to be coordinated and timed according to the task at hand. Everything has a sequence. For example, you wouldn't frame a house before pouring the foundation, just as you can't paint the walls and ceilings until the drywall is installed and textured. It's a lot like dominoes, and if some dominoes are missing, the whole sequence fails.

Of course, some of the delays are out of anyone's control, but some aren't. I remember at one point where the carrying costs of our company got so high that every single day of operation was costing in the neighborhood of $30,000. Yes, any day without progress, regardless of the reason, whether it was due to a holiday, bad weather, or a random Sunday, meant that we were essentially throwing $30,000 in the trash. I got frequent stomachaches.

The reason it's so easy to get behind, and that the delays can mushroom, is that each house you're building requires that you coordinate numerous components, materials, and contractors. They all need to be synchronized to keep the construction process on track. That's a challenge with many tasks that appear to be out of your control. But when you multiply that by however many steps and houses you're building at one time, the situation can quickly get out of hand.

Managing movements and efficiency is a talent. I've been in many industries, including the restaurant business, where I remember how challenging it was to orchestrate every single dish to be delivered to every person at a table simultaneously, and to have each course perfectly timed for each person at every table. Ask a chef and they'll tell you. The same is true here but since nobody is screaming for their missing salad, it's easier to ignore the accumulated missing pieces that eventually turn into a real problem. Enforcing schedules from each independent contractor at the exact time when you need them is no picnic. Fortunately, as with every other science, if you apply talent, discipline, persistence, and perseverance, and you want it bad enough, you'll get there. There is, in fact, a know-how to every art form, which all great operators and industry leaders possess. Is it difficult? Yes. Is it possible? Absolutely!!

Because even when you coordinate your construction process well and you have all your ducks in an impressive row, things can still go awry. Maybe your foundation guy fell behind by a few days and then it rained and the framer that had been scheduled couldn't do the work then, so you missed your window of opportunity to get that work done. You then have to reconstruct your whole schedule because that requires your plumber and electrician to come later, once the framer is rescheduled, and so on and so forth. Of course, the ideal date for those contractors to return may not align perfectly with their availability, so you may end up waiting a few extra days or even weeks because of another job they are committed to. Coordinating all of the crews becomes a juggling act of mass proportions, which is harder the more projects you have going at once.

Managing multiple contractors and dealing with weather interference can upend your well-planned schedule. Sure, it will eventually get done, but likely not on your original timetable, which eats into your profit margin the longer the house takes to complete. But believe it or not, if you put your heart and soul into it, it is very possible to eventually establish a rhythm that only generates very small tolerable delays.

Repetition is the mother of all profits

Home building is, at its heart, a creative business. It's all about creating something from nothing. The opportunity to envision and develop new designs, new floor plans, and new styles is part of the fun for those of you who have an artistic side. What's exciting is the chance to try new approaches, to invent, and to innovate. What's new and different is often fun and exciting.

Accept that every time you change some aspect of the design, whether it's as simple as the exterior elevation/façade or kitchen layout, there is a learning curve that costs you money. And when you modify something more involved, like the home's entire floor plan, there will be more of everything—more costs, more time required, more variation in quality, and more variation in results. Unless you are a custom home builder or focusing strictly on multimillion-dollar luxury homes, too much creativity can be counterproductive.

I come back to the analogy of being a doctor. You may get general medical training, but if you're a cardiac surgeon for several years and then decide to switch overnight to neurosurgery, you're not going to be as skilled a neurosurgeon at the outset. You have to learn the intricacies of how the brain works in order to master it like you did the heart.

Obviously not to that level but the same logic applies with home building. Once you perfect a particular style and floor plan, you get better and faster because you know it inside and out. You know where problems are likely to arise and can avoid them. You easily spot any errors and can anticipate the issues that may arise, as well as the objections. Your contractors also learn the ins and outs of one particular plan and the better and faster they get, the more money you can make.

Although replicating the same design may seem boring, that monotony is what will make you more money if you intend to achieve any level of volume. Every time you try something new, there is a learning curve attached that can slow your progress and potentially reduce your profit margin.

Everything that is new shakes up the system you've honed. It destabilizes it, whether you change the plan, the design, the price point, the neighborhood, the general contractor, or the architect.

You have to then relearn how that plan can work best in a new location. If you're not a custom home builder where the buyer is paying to innovate, you do not want to reinvent the wheel on every house. Once you understand what works and what you're best at, those types of homes become what we call your "bread and butter." They are the type of homes you can build in your sleep and while you probably won't make a windfall on every sale, you'll have more predictability in your business. So, become great at one thing before you jump to the next in order to better leverage your expertise.

Think about it: scaling a business is every entrepreneur's dream. It's how empires are built, and fortunes are made. But that concept requires repetition. You create it, you produce it, you package it, and you sell it, over and over. Microsoft created its Office Suite and sells copies of the same product day in and day out. Tesla does not redesign every single car they produce; instead, they come up with that successful model and build it over and over. They created a product they can sell repeatedly that doesn't need customization. So, unless you want to spend a fortune redesigning things, try to repeat what works.

Granted, this may not necessarily be what you end up doing, and that's where selecting a model becomes important, as long as you understand where you want to go. For example, the approach we took at Tricon was different because our model was more of an architectural boutique firm, building semi-custom homes. Although we did a lot of repetition, we also built many homes only once. This was based on a buyer's requirements and other times just for fun, but we knew that recreating a design each time as opposed to building the same one 1,000 times was more work and less profit. Had we done that, we would have made a ton of money much faster, though it would not have been as creatively satisfying.

If you look at the business model of the largest real estate developers, you will see that they offer fewer floor plan options, fewer packages to select from, and fewer options overall. The higher the volume of construction, generally, the lower the number of design options offered. They take a cookie cutter approach on purpose. They become a machine, even designing homes to fit a precise lot size.

Project managers

As I've mentioned repeatedly, hiring a superintendent to be on-site at all times can help ensure quality work, but don't be surprised if it becomes challenging to find a construction manager who is great at everything that this job demands. And if you get lucky enough to find one, hold on to that person! The qualifications are numerous, almost as well-rounded as an owner. Someone with that sense of ownership, respect, and appreciation for the business without actually owning it, is almost too good to be true. This is one of those jobs that requires multiple aptitudes, and you'll commonly land a candidate with one or two of the qualities but rarely all. You may end up with someone who's either very detailed but unreliable or reliable but not focused or managerial but too tough on the workers. Or maybe they are amazingly personable and customer service-oriented to work with your buyers, but way too relaxed with workers. Or highly technical but incapable of meeting with prospects, or good at all these things but horrible organization skills.

Then there's the great manager who is horrible with estimates, numbers, and paperwork, or the one who'll speak too much on your behalf, with a tendency to give away a lot of freebies to buyers that you never agreed to and will end up costing you extra. You want someone balanced who is able to follow directions, to pay close attention to the work being done, and be willing to correct workers, as necessary. Someone who is nice but firm with contractors. They also need to be organized and on top of all the paperwork that is part of the process—a good scheduler and a personable representative of your company. You need a superintendent with a personality who can make buyers feel good about the work being done on their homes. Since this is not an employee sitting next to you in your office who you can constantly watch over, finding this self-motivated, well-balanced, focused, hardworking, ethical, passionate individual who will take pride in monitoring your house is easier said than done. These individuals are needles in a haystack. The answer, oftentimes, is to do a lot of training in order to get them accustomed to the way you expect things to be handled.

Homeowner Associations

Homeowner Associations (HOAs) are important to be aware of and understand before you ever buy a property. The purpose of an HOA is to enforce a set of rules and guidelines within any given neighborhood or subdivision that will help maintain uniformity, upkeep value, consistency, and order for residents. There are actually two aspects to be aware of with HOAs: 1) whether there is one already in place in the neighborhood or community and if there's not 2) whether you need to create one for the community you're building.

Is there an active HOA in place?

As part of the purchase process, you need to learn whether there is an existing HOA. This information is shown on your title commitment and, surprisingly, every now and then, in some very old neighborhoods, it's not always recorded properly, so you need to investigate on your own to be sure either way. You don't want to be surprised to find out that there is an HOA that you weren't aware of and that, consequently, limits what you can build. Or that you're responsible for paying a monthly fee you hadn't counted on. HOAs are recorded on your Schedule B, where the exclusions to your title work are shown.

Next, investigate whether any recorded HOAs are active or inactive. Some have ceased to be active if the term of performance has expired or if no one is managing it. But if the HOA is active, you'll want to ask to see:

- The charter—current directors
- Background information
- The stated purpose of this particular HOA
- Details regarding fees
- Details regarding restrictions
- The existence of committees, such as architectural
- Contact information

Once you have those details, you can investigate whether the HOA could interfere or reject your proposed plans. Then get in touch and discuss your project to learn if there are any objections or restrictions that would impact your property.

Do you need one?

On the flipside, if you're building on raw land with nothing of that nature attached to the property, you'll also want to determine if you need to create one. If you're building a single house or a group of homes facing an existing street or block, you don't need one. There is no reason to have one.

However, if you're building your own development on, say, a few acres of land and are building a community from scratch, particularly if it's gated, you will need to set up an HOA. As part of the project, you'll be responsible for installing the infrastructure, such as sewer connections, the plumbing, the streets, fences, as well as some landscaping, perhaps. These all incorporate common areas requiring regular maintenance provided initially by you, the developer, which will then be handed over to an HOA to manage once the community is completed and sold.

On top of maintenance and upkeep, you will have created a set of rules and guidelines with a level of consistency that you'll want to retain in order to maintain property values. Basically, with the assistance of an attorney or a management company specialist, you'll create a document to be recorded for the benefit of homeowners that indicate the standards you set, cover the rules of the new subdivision, and disclose the yearly membership fees associated with ownership for the upkeep.

HOAs are normally responsible for managing things like cutting the grass and maintaining any outdoor common areas, like a broken front gate. They also take care of salting and snowplowing roadways, where applicable, or escrowing money for property taxes and utilities for common areas, or any repairs associated with the development. The document also outlines what is permitted and what is not. I'm not going to tell you what you should include—attorneys are best for that—but I'll give you a few items to consider. For example, can you paint the exterior of your home in any color or only in the ones identified by the HOA? Can homes be used for short-term rentals, such as Airbnb and VRBO? Can a homeowner park a travel trailer in their driveway during the winter? Can signs be placed in front of homes? Can commercial businesses, either low or high traffic, such as bakeries or shops, be operated in the community? Can you remodel the exterior of your house any style you want or only the ones allowed? Can you install additional fencing and, if yes, where and up to what height? These are just a few situations to consider, but there are many others.

Do keep in mind that the more restrictive the rules, the more they need to make sense according to the type of development or you could end up affecting the appeal of the community. Be careful not to go overboard. Once drafted, you'll record your HOA document so that buyers understand what the rules are, and then you'll provide it to the management company so everyone there is informed as well.

CHAPTER 10

Pricing Properties

One of the secrets you need to master in this industry is how to price a home. There is a constant struggle between parties negotiating a high-stake transaction, where builders want to get more, buyers hope to pay less, and brokers need to make deals. Pricing is ultimately what makes or breaks sales. Where do you start and where do you draw the line? How do you play this poker game? You don't want to lose sales, but you also don't want to give away your product. How do you determine what the true and fair value is?

The answer is: Know what you have and know what the buyers' other alternatives are. You must have a clear understanding of the value that you bring to the table and be aware of how your home compares to the competition. Be well-informed and you'll know when to stand firm and when it makes sense to give out those special concessions. Evaluate the differences between your product and everything else out there that is in direct competition with you.

When the offers come in, it's your job to educate buyers about your amenities. When offers are low, one of the things I do is to ask how they arrived at their number. Many times it is not justified and the explanation provided makes no sense other than that they are looking for a good deal. Fortunately, good deals have no correlation with value and that's what you need to focus on. Once you're able to separate yourself from the pack, you will have more success bringing in the types of offers that your house deserves.

Of course, if it's a seller's market, you'll always have more control, just as buyers will take over when there is excess inventory. Ultimately, every home sale should be a win-win situation. As mediators say, the best mediations are the ones where no one got exactly what they wanted, but everyone walked away happy and satisfied with the outcome. This is also true in home sales.

Pricing is both a science and an art. You need to be informed about what's going on in your market in order to price accurately. That gets easier as you gain experience and forge more relationships with other industry leaders you can learn from. Do your research and draw your own conclusions.

But you should try to tap into the collective wisdom of as many information sources as you can while you're building your business. That's where the art comes in. You can then apply your own experience and perspective to decide what patterns you're seeing and how your company should take advantage of opportunities that are emerging.

Overpricing is just as counterproductive as underpricing, which can make you lose prospects and waste valuable marketing time.

Don't build based on media reports

Now, there's a big difference between gathering information and processing it yourself based on what you know, versus allowing what the news is reporting to drive your business. Don't make decisions based solely on what you're reading, watching, and hearing on the news. Don't adapt your price points in reaction to something the news is reporting as fact, because the truth is, you know more than the reporters about what's happening specifically in the home building market in your area.

PRICING PROPERTIES

When we got into the home building business back in the 1990s, typical price points were very different, of course. I think the median price was under $200,000, with many of the homes we were initially building in the $120,000s or $130,000s in what was considered a transitional neighborhood; prices were considerably lower. (Today those same homes are in the $400,000s, just for comparison.) If we were to build these same homes in developments that have now been revitalized, we would then be talking about $800,000s due to land appreciation alone. Over time, the average prices have risen and little by little they more than doubled. But back to the point, which is that only a few years later, our homes were being priced in the $300,000s because the neighborhood is no longer considered transitional; it's established and more desirable.

Our initial strategy was "saturation," meaning focusing only on a couple of neighborhoods at a time in order to build a name and make more impact. As we expected, the land quickly got more expensive as these submarkets began looking better thanks to our own redevelopment efforts. It was as if we were the cause of our own land costs increasing, as each round of land acquisitions was pricier than the last. It became funny to hear land sellers say how their lot was now worth more because of all the new construction happening around them and I would answer: "Of course, I know, we are the ones doing all of that development." We created that demand as we were building more projects, more developments, and all of a sudden, land prices had risen considerably.

Everyone—brokers, agents, other builders—started telling me that the market was hottest in lower-priced homes under $200,000. To be able to build at that price point meant going to some more remote and speculative areas. They told me I needed to find cheaper land to build on, outside my target neighborhoods, because "this first-time buyer market was so hot" and otherwise I would "miss out."

Feeling the pressure, I decided to try to get into the entry-level market, to try to diversify my portfolio. But I was chasing the market. I tried to go after lower-priced homes when that wasn't my specialty or my short-term goal. I found some properties, developed them, built on them, and within a year, that market had changed yet again. The entry-level price points had become much more competitive, so it became difficult to make a profit.

Meanwhile, homes at the higher end, where we had previously been specializing before I had become distracted by the supposed hot entry-level market, had gotten much more popular. These were in the $500,000 range at the time, compatible with today's $1 million or $1.5 million properties.

That meant that because I had been chasing the market, I had several properties priced in the $190,000s and low $200,000s that were not selling. My solution? Buy some lots in the $500,000 price points to go after homes selling at $600,000 and $700,000, where I thought that market was headed.

Within a year or two, of course, the market shifted once more back to favor homes in the mid-$200,000s. Since I had to get rid of my properties to be able to stock up on the higher-end lots, I didn't have any more in that range.

I was chasing the market and losing. So, don't do what I did—don't chase it. Build what you want to build because you like that price point, style, or location, and become a true specialist in it, so that you understand it better than any other builder in your area.

A home is not a product that can be produced overnight. The market will change, rotate, and fluctuate faster than you can shift gears and take advantage of what's now hot. Don't listen to others who will whisper in your ear that you should get into a different type of home. Stick with your specialty. Don't worry about what others are doing.

Half of success in this business is due to luck. The other half is timing. If you stick with what you do best, eventually the market will come to you and you'll be able to take advantage. Wait for the market to shift in your direction. Don't try to catch it.

Also realize that the media is not in the business of selling homes. Much of what the media reports is fear-based. That is their business—to capture attention, by whatever means necessary in some situations—to amplify, dramatize, exaggerate, and whatever else to influence your decision-making. You may hear the market is crashing, the market is booming, it's a seller's market, it's a buyer's market. Don't listen. Ignore it, or you will begin to make bad decisions. It happened to me, so I'm warning you based on my personal experience.

Instead, focus on understanding what's going on in your neck of the woods based on tangible economic data, not what the anchor on tonight's newscast who likely lacks any home building experience is telling you. Focus on your numbers. Focus on your goals. Focus on what you can control in your business, not external factors over which you have no control.

So, what should you pay attention to? What I call the fundamentals in our industry.

Watching the market and listening to the signs

As humans, we tend to ignore the issues that can actually make a difference in the outcome of our business decisions. Most people assume that the global economy, or more general trends, drive your local market. That's incorrect. The home building industry is driven by very basic fundamental aspects.

The rental market

One of the most important signs I watch is the rental market. Renters are future home buyers; they are the raw materials, effectively. So, I watch how my community's rental business is growing, how rents are increasing or changing, and what type of construction is going up, because that will impact future buyers' willingness to move. You want the rental business to be healthy and strong, to feed you with people graduating to home ownership.

In particular, I watch what apartment and commercial developers are doing, rather than home builders, because the larger national home builders are creating their own "city size" master-planned communities and not evaluating the markets and neighborhoods where I am. On the other hand, apartment and commercial builders are operating all around me and analyzing everything that's going on around me, only that they have more resources invested in demographics and market research. They have a much better grasp of what's coming and what's happening in the areas where guys like me operate.

If you monitor rent prices and increases, you should also become intimately familiar with cost-of-living ratios and at what point it becomes feasible for renters to consider buying.

I used to joke about watching the area's wedding industry closely but, funny enough, it was a helpful guide, since weddings are often a precursor to a home purchase. Once couples get married, they often start thinking next about buying a house. Some want to start a family and the common assumption is that families want and deserve to live in houses.

Growth of your city

Another important factor is the growth of the population in your area. How many people are moving into your city? Or, how many are leaving? Those are very important numbers to stay on top of.

The number of folks moving into town is more relevant to your business than what's going on in another part of the world. How many families are moving in, where they are predominantly coming from, what's driving them there, what neighborhoods they are targeting, and what size units they are renting or buying are most relevant to you. Three-bedroom? Four-bedroom? All of those renters will eventually convert to home buyers. Pay attention to some of the metrics related to your city to get a better grasp of what might be coming down the road for your home building business.

PRICING PROPERTIES

Local industry performance

How are local companies and industries doing in general? Every city is strong in one or more industries, so how are they doing?

For example, although it has become much more diversified, Texas is still very energy-focused, with oil and gas in its roots. Houston alone has one of the largest medical centers in the world, the second-largest port, a solid manufacturing base, a rising petrochemical industry, and a number of headquarters of financial corporations. This helps both attract new residents and reduce the chance that the city will suddenly be impacted by the performance of one specific industry.

Similarly, Wilmington, Delaware, has long been known as a banking and corporate haven, which has led to a strong legal industry, and the presence of the DuPont company and its various divisions helps reduce the chances of an unexpected downturn there. New York City is another example of a fairly diversified market base, which helps keep demand for housing strong.

What does your area have as far as industry?

Employment

Employment is perhaps the number one driver of incoming residents, so you'll also want to watch those numbers. What is the local employment (or unemployment) rate and is it trending up or down? What kinds of industries are moving in and what positions are being created, with what levels of salaries? This is important as it helps determine the type of inventory that the city can absorb, and the salary levels will determine a consumer's ability to save money for the down payment required.

Interest rates

Although not a local issue, mortgage interest rates also impact homebuying. Interest rates dictate your monthly payment and the price of a house you can buy. As rates go up, the size of your buyer pool shrinks in the short-term as families decide to keep renting until rates stabilize. As rental property loans mature, these commercial property owners must refinance at higher rates, and rents rise again and start catching up and surpassing mortgages. Then renters once again explore buying.

Across the country, in addition to many other benefits of home ownership, it is often cheaper to buy a three-bedroom or four-bedroom home than it is to rent a two-bedroom apartment. Your mortgage payment, including principal and interest, insurance, and property taxes together are often lower than paying rent. It doesn't make sense to rent given that situation, and with homeownership you get to build wealth and save money while permanently locking down the monthly payment. But in the short-term, when interest rates rise faster than rent increases, renting appears more affordable.

Affordability

What medium-priced homes cost in comparison to local salaries is another metric to study. There are periods of time when that fine balance can go off track. This can be due to a variety of reasons, like a city experiencing rapid growth can cause a faster-than-normal increase in property values. An economic boom, an unusually large population influx, or the relocation of a large headquarters will cause a short-term reaction that creates a shortage in housing availability. San Francisco at one point, and more recently Austin, are good examples of where the housing market got temporarily out of whack. Affordability became unattainable when the price of houses rose far above what the average employee was making in that city.

Everyone wanted to be there, until things got so expensive that there was a small housing bubble forming. That bubble expanded until buyers could no longer afford what was left in the market, and then it popped and prices adjusted. Other times the market can go in the opposite direction, with house prices stabilizing and even temporarily dropping, until buyers grab an opportunity and start buying homes up, driving prices up again. That is part of the normal housing cycle driven by supply and demand.

Access to credit

Most of us don't pay cash for a home. We need access to credit through mortgages, which is part of the system in the US. The federal laws and regulators who govern these types of loans often make adjustments. When these requirements change, these policies might either get easier at times or harder to meet, depending on a number of conditions.

When the rules become more flexible, more people qualify and therefore more people buy; the same happens the other way around. It's important for those rules to remain well balanced in order to maintain a healthy economy, where people who qualify for the purchase of a home can indeed afford it, and can meet the right criteria of home ownership.

Inventory

What is currently available for sale in your market is another factor to watch. That is, what is the inventory like? How much is out there? What price points have too much for sale and which others have next to nothing? How many are completed and how many under construction in the pipeline? That can tell you what people can afford and where demand currently is.

This must be measured in relation to speed of absorption, meaning the number of homes available compared to how many are being sold each month. If ten homes are available and ten sell in a month, you have 100 percent absorption. There is enough demand for what's currently available in that instance.

Permits-in-progress

I watch inventory counts along with permits-in-progress to see what will be coming on the market in the next few months. Inventory is what is available today and permits-in-progress is a measure of where builders think the market is headed. What they are currently building signals what they think the market wants and what the market is projected to do.

Finding that information isn't hard. You can look at your city's website to learn not only what's being permitted, as far as individual homes, but also what is already re-platted, as well as which re-plats are in progress and where builders are splitting them into residential or commercial lots. That can tell you a lot in and of itself.

Permitting cycle

Regarding how many permits are being processed, the size of the city and the regulations and steps required affect how long it takes for a permit to be approved. Long permitting cycles can affect the pace at which a project can be developed and how quickly houses can be built. That can also affect any trends you think you may be seeing. If the permitting cycle is going to take, say, six months to a year, be sure to factor that into your assessment, understanding that the homes being built won't be on the market immediately.

Take into account how long your typical permit takes as you look ahead to the coming months.

Again, these are data points based on actual numbers, rather than media reports, overblown projections, or dire predictions. They are based on facts, not extrapolations, which can be shaped to fit the source's narrative. And if you pay attention to these signs, you'll get a heads up to what changes may be coming your way that could impact your company.

Believe me, the signs are there. At times, it's natural to be overly optimistic, borderline in denial. For example, when you're in growth

PRICING PROPERTIES

mode and the data tells you it's not the best moment to expand, your tendency might be to ignore it and proceed. But if you start seeing interest rates creeping up, rents starting to be discounted, unemployment on the rise, and inventories of houses expanding in different neighborhoods, those are signs of an economy in transition and you'll want to react accordingly to protect your business. Pay attention to the signs, not the TV or news reports.

Offering a bonus to buyer's agent (BTBA) is a related sign that builders may be getting nervous. When sellers start to offer bonus payments to get agents to bring buyers through houses, to boost traffic, you know that builders are motivated. Those BTSAs may also be accompanied by discounting and price reductions.

Pre-sell or not?

Deciding whether to pre-sell a house can be a confusing dilemma, starting with the fact that the term "pre-sold" is itself broad. But there are also different angles and perspectives from which to evaluate the effects of selling a house at an early stage. First of all, at what stage of the construction is it considered pre-sold? Before breaking ground, or at ten percent, twenty percent, or even at ninety percent of completion? The technical answer can vary depending on who you ask, and I won't go down that rabbit hole. We could claim that selling a house prior to 100 percent of completion is considered pre-sold, but it can also sell at any stage of the process, so instead of attempting to define what it means to pre-sell, let's focus on the subject of how to identify the ideal stage of construction to sell a house according to your business goals.

It's clear that for many reasons, as a low-volume, high-end luxury custom home builder, it's beneficial to pre-sell. Custom homes are designed and built for a client, hence the word custom. They are normally complicated and pricey, so it makes all the sense in the world to create these unique luxury items to the specifications of a single buyer. But when your goal is to become more of a semi-custom builder who pretends to achieve a certain level of volume, not so much. While you might assume that pre-selling a home would be a safe and smart move because it guarantees you have a buyer, it might actually be a pain in the neck. That's because instead of being able to efficiently operate according to your standard specifications, features, and at your own speed, when you have a buyer involved early on, you may experience more interruptions that will require their approval and participation at almost every step. They become your boss to a large extent, and unless it's a multimillion-dollar project, it might not be worth the trouble.

For example, I can build six houses in the $400,000 price range without a buyer or one with a buyer in the same time frame, so the "opportunity cost" could be tremendous. The reason that it takes much more time with a buyer is that they will have questions, emails, meetings with your design department, changes, and other delays to ensure that they get the house they want. You have to work at their pace when you pre-sell, which may not be in your company's best interest. Your buyers may bring you fixtures they hand-selected and will ask you to install them instead of what you had already chosen. They may point out small errors you had already identified and planned to correct in due time, or simple issues that will slow you down because they want them addressed *now*, as opposed to according to your original schedule. So, avoid it if you can unless you have a healthy profit margin built in that allows you to hold your buyer's hand at every step of the way. The biggest intangible cost is that a buyer may very well consume so much of your time that it will distract you and your staff from the rest of your projects. We experienced that many times where all of a sudden, a dozen of our other homes fell behind schedule for attending to one single picky buyer.

If you end up having to pre-sell, be very clear in your agreement what your procedures are and spell out how involved your buyer is permitted to be. Be super clear about decisions that they may help make and those they cannot, because I can assure you that even when you provide strict written, signed, and agreed-upon rules, guidelines, and procedures establishing those boundaries, they will be broken. Once a buyer feels that the house is being built for them, it is likely that they'll try to justify why their involvement is necessary, putting you in constant struggles and negotiations through the whole process instead of making progress in the house. I've had many buyers over the years that regardless of signing an ironclad agreement stating the rules of the game, they figured out how to take control of the job site.

There are different levels of customization. You can allow a total custom home from the ground up, including the floor plan, the elevations, the design, the styles, the finishes—everything. And at that level of customization, you should be charging a premium price.

Or you can sell a semi-custom home, where you specify the floor plan and the buyer can only select the finishes, the colors, and the stones for each item individually or as one of your available pre-selected options. You might allow them to make small changes, like moving a nonbearing wall in the closet. But there should also be limits to what they can modify in the plans. Stick to your business model and don't adapt to everyone's needs. The more you limit their participation, the faster you'll move along with your homes.

Without clear limits and boundaries, you will often find buyers talking to your contractors directly, asking them questions, and requesting small changes they are not authorized to request.

That's what pre-selling can often lead to—buyers trying to drive the building process. You want to avoid that as much as possible.

Also, you can easily make small accidental adjustments and changes when you don't have a buyer. For example, maybe you discover that your flooring team used a different color than you had specified. It looks good, it's just not the exact shade you had envisioned. To save money, and because it looks fine, you keep it. No one will ever know it wasn't the stain you had chosen. However, if you had pre-sold it and the wrong stain color was used, you would have to pay the contractor to redo it to match what the buyer had specified.

While there are negatives, there are also advantages to pre-selling.

The biggest advantage is that pre-selling a home removes the risk that the house won't sell, and it makes lenders and investors feel safer. It reassures everyone involved that you made good choices. You don't have to worry anymore about selling it because somebody wants it. Someone is willing to pay the price you've asked. They have validated your product. You've locked in your sales price and received a deposit from a buyer, so it's no longer a speculative transaction.

Of course, the one downside of this is if the market takes off during the next few months. If prices start rising dramatically and as you finish building the house you discover you could have sold it for more if you had waited, you effectively lost money. By locking in a buyer early on, you eliminate most risk, but you also eliminate any upside potential you could have taken advantage of. This situation was a reality for me many times during improving markets, including during Covid, when we had contracts in place and the market went up $30,000 or $40,000 per house as families decided they wanted to move. Those pre-sales cost my company a lot of money.

Unless you get a very large, non-refundable deposit up-front, which is not always easy on lower-priced homes, I personally dislike pre-selling because you get the worst of both worlds. You lose out on any upside potential by early contracts, but your buyer can also walk away at any time if they're willing to lose their small deposit in the event the market crashes. Truthfully, while you've reduced your risk through a pre-sale, you haven't entirely eliminated it.

But should you pre-sell? There's no wrong answer as long as you know what each of these mean. A lot has to do with your objectives and with your business model. If you're building one, two, or three homes a year, yes, pre-selling can be a smart choice. You can devote more time to your buyers, you can build pricier homes, you can give them more choices, more decisions, and focus on each of them.

However, if your business model is based on volume, where you're building twenty, fifty, or more houses a year, pre-selling homes in the early stages is less feasible. You simply have less time and attention available to service your buyers when you're building so many homes at once.

Think like a buyer, not a builder

As you get consumed by managing people and deadlines, it's easy to get wrapped up in activities and overwhelming schedules. Understand that building a house is a lot like those restaurants that show the chefs cooking behind a clear glass barrier—everyone walking by can see what you're doing, see what the place looks like, check out your activities, and how clean and orderly you're keeping the space. You'll have neighbors, uninvited guests, brokers, agents, as well as potential buyers. Unbeknown to you, they'll start to make judgments about how you run your business based on what they see in that environment you've created. It's smart to keep things looking organized and attractive at all times as much as possible, more as you would see in retail or in a boutique with walking traffic versus in a closed warehouse operation where messes can be hidden away. This sounds easier said than done because building this product can be a total mess, but that's precisely why it's important. It says a lot about how you run your entire company.

Although they may know next to nothing about your business or the process of building a home, visitors will start to develop opinions about your professionalism based solely on what they can see, and we should not forget to consider the customer's perspective. For example, let's say you had a little mishap and a duct was installed in the wrong place, so you have to break up a few things to re-route it. Or there was a leak forcing you to remove some already installed items. Or for whatever reason, the electrician had to re-run some cables, leaving behind a bunch of unidentified holes in different walls, and now the so called "New House" starts looking damaged or messy with debris and holes everywhere. Although this is completely normal within the standard process, the average consumer doesn't know that.

People who happen to walk through the house may wonder, "What's going on with the craftsmanship of this house? Why is there so much trash and all these random holes everywhere?" Now, as the builder, you know this is not a big deal and you put it at the end of your list of things to do so as to avoid interrupting other activities going on. "I'll have my sheetrock guy do it later," you say to yourself.

Bad idea.

Just as chefs clean the kitchen as they go, you as a home builder need to make your repairs and clean up the messes in the house *as you go*. Otherwise, the space starts looking like a nightmare. The impression you give is that you're less organized, less competent. As a result, those people will share the wrong opinion about your organization. The entire building process is definitely a disaster but don't ignore messes. Pick up the trash frequently. Have your workers clean up as they finish each stage. This demonstrates to anyone walking by at any stage of the construction that you are taking great care to build a quality house. You're not building a sloppy one. Optics can often shape public opinion.

This activity is a permanent uphill battle that requires constant effort. Many workers who normally eat their breakfast or lunch at the site leave their trash all around the place, and it's your job to enforce that they clean up after themselves. Also, you must make an effort to address small details, and in addition to presenting an image of cleanliness and care, for example, we placed plywood on the ground in exterior traffic areas where it could get muddy after it rains, so that there is easy access without stepping on mud. You can comfortably walk the property and visitors' shoes, particularly ladies in high heels, will thank you for it. We would pride ourselves in removing trash daily and patching up repairs as we went along. You have to be proactive or else your project can become a pigsty almost overnight.

The ideal time to put your home on the market

This might be a bit redundant, going very much hand in hand with the earlier topic addressing whether to pre-sell or not, but let's discuss this from the optimum marketing perspective, as opposed to the builder-model perspective. The question here is more relevant for *speculative builders* who chose to design and break ground without a buyer, but now the issue is, at what point should I list the house? When do I begin my marketing efforts and what are the pros and cons at different stages? Their graph is simple—the longer and further you can advance without a buyer, the speedier and more efficiently you can finish it. Unfortunately, also by waiting until the very end, once the house is completed, touched up, fully staged, and looking perfect, it gives you little time to find a buyer.

There are several ways to evaluate this. Most builders will probably list the house the moment they break ground, to avoid wasting the possibility of missing out on a single buyer. However, that's deceiving because unless you already have a very similar model home available for them to see, they'll find it difficult to understand exactly what you're building. Floor plans and photos are great tools but might not be enough. Buyers rarely have the ability to appreciate spaces without touching, walking, and feeling them. So, by trying to promote too soon, you might actually waste time and energy meeting with prospects and not get very far. Is it smart to start driving traffic early on, while the project is still less than attractive, without fences or landscaping, no appliances, the absence of a few sconces, missing light fixtures, and no final coat of fresh paint?

This is a double-edged sword. It might feel like by rushing these efforts you are gaining time, but you may only be wasting perfectly qualified candidates who were unable to see the vision of a 100 percent final product. Sort of like going on a first date and meeting someone who's all sweaty, has no personal hygiene, dressed awful, has messy hair, with zero effort. Will there be a second date? Probably not. This doesn't mean that every buyer requires that perfect presentation, I am only providing scenarios for you to consider. Ultimately the decision you make has more to do with your own instinct and gut feeling than anything else.

However, the slower the market, the more perfect the house needs to look. Yes, as inventory grows, the more perfect your house needs to be in order to stand out. So, we go back to evaluating what else is on the market. If there's a lot of finished inventory available, you might not need to rush listing your home, but if there's nothing else out there, prospects will buy sooner than later, so list now.

My personal preference is to avoid putting my houses on the market until they're about eighty to ninety percent complete. Yes, they may still not look perfect but I'm comfortable with that gamble assuming that they always look as clean and organized as possible until they are finally staged. By this time, there are few things left to complete and still time to make small buyer requests, but it's important to always explain the details of what is yet to be done.

> You can always use changes and upgrades as negotiating points with buyers, as opposed to cash discounts, to get the sale. We typically don't make a whole lot of money on those, but we offer them to expedite a sale. That may mean that we'll paint the walls a different color, add crown molding to a room, build some additional cabinets, tear out and replace a backsplash, or maybe redo some tile in the bathroom in order to seal the deal with a buyer if that's what it takes.

Another factor to observe is buyers' timing. The bulk of buyers begin their new home search approximately forty-five to sixty days out from when they need it, often because they are moving into town or that's when their apartment lease ends. Knowing that, you can see how by listing six months out, you might not be wasting too many prospects.

Negotiating with buyers

How much I'm willing to negotiate and stretch that rubber band, other than for market conditions, is often dictated by my own company's situation at that particular moment. As I go along developing projects, I'll consider what my company's circumstances are—are our finances stable enough that I don't have to take that first low offer so seriously, or do I need to not be so picky? What is the market looking like? Is demand picking up or are buyers backing away? Determining whether you can afford to let an offer go is the first step in the negotiation. It will tell you whether you can play tough or if you need to be more flexible with your demands. There are moments in time when sellers can almost name their price and get it, because of temporary house shortages where people line up to buy houses in bidding wars. But that doesn't last, as the market constantly shifts; you may need to adjust your own psychology and expectations.

A common mistake that I see smaller builders make is placing more importance on the profitability of a single home than on the health and needs of their company. This puts their entire business at risk by not accepting offers because they are not at the anticipated price. That can be dangerous.

I run every one of my firms as a game of chess. My firm is the king and my homes are the rest of the pieces—the knights, the rooks, the pawns. Sometimes I have to let go of one of those pieces in order to save my king and continue on with the game, just as I must let go of a house even if it's not at the price I wanted for the sake of the company. Maybe I need that equity back for the cash flow, or I need to clear a line of credit that matured or pay some urgent bills in order to allow me to continue in the game. Your company is more important than any one sale.

On the other hand, if you have seven offers and two houses to sell, you obviously don't have to be as flexible. You don't have to be in a hurry to give in, or to agree to a buyer's terms asap because you have options. You have other buyers ready to work with you. But if the reverse is true and you have seven houses and only one under contract, you may need to take steps to drum up some interest.

Your pricing will tell you within thirty days if your house is overpriced. If you don't have traffic, you don't have showings, or prospects, or offers, you will have to face the fact that the market is telling you that your house is not generating interest at your asking price.

You've probably heard the adage that the first offer is your best offer, and that's usually true, though it's not a rule. So, keeping in mind that the pricier the house, the smaller your buyer pool, you may want to seriously consider that first offer and negotiate it until you make it work. There may not be that many other buyers in your price range, depending on the market, so before you reject it or try to play hardball, reflect on your company's finances and circumstances.

When an offer makes sense, don't get so caught up in trying to maximize your profits. Nobody ever went bankrupt by turning a profit. So, don't get greedy trying to break records unless it's happening on its own. Sure, you may want to make $60,000 and instead this time you'll make $40,000, but at least you're in the black.

A fairly common phenomenon is when an offer comes in so fast that you think it is a sign of many more to come, so you get stubborn and don't agree to provide any concessions. And then no other offers come in and your house sits on the market for months.

Don't dig in your heels so deep you can't take a step back if you need to. Because it's possible you just got lucky, and that one quick offer may be the only one you get. Be reasonable.

Treat every offer with respect. Getting an offer quickly doesn't always mean that more are coming, nor does it mean that it's a bad offer. It may be in your best interests to negotiate and take it. Timing is a critical factor in this market and over time, a house that sits becomes stale. Usually that starts happening after ninety days of completion. By then, everyone in the market at that price point has seen it and the fact that it's still there suggests that there could be something wrong with it. Even worse, you're accumulating costs. To counteract that, you'll want to quickly adjust your price. You want to try to accelerate sales at this point, because every month you hold it, the greater your chance of having to hold it another month, further eating into your profits. It becomes harder to recoup your investment the longer it sits.

But price isn't the only factor to try to negotiate. Explain your house's features. The home's features can have a big impact on its appeal and yet many builders neglect to properly explain the contents to their agent or on their listing, so the buyer doesn't realize many details about what the house contains. Take time to explain the brands you chose and why, the finishes, the selections, the inspiration, the type of flooring, the type of windows, the brand of lighting.

Create a spec sheet summarizing all of the features your home offers and that differentiate it from others in the area, so that when people are touring other homes, they can more easily compare the two and recognize the value you're offering them.

Even if a house is absolutely perfect for them, few buyers will ever admit that. Instead, they'll tell you, "We like it, but we wish it had X. But if you sell it at this price, we can live with it as-is." Knowing that they are going to try this tactic, you have to be able to differentiate and articulate what it is that your house offers compared to others they may be considering.

On an individual level, you can often have success by listening to their objections clearly and then offering to change what you can. For example, maybe a buyer doesn't like your color scheme—too much grey, perhaps—or they don't like the countertops you chose. Once you know their specific objection, you can decide if you want to make that change for them. Yes, it will cost you a little money, but making a sale sooner will also save you carrying costs. You have to weigh the two.

While you don't necessarily want to receive low-ball offers from buyers, don't discourage them. I'm never afraid of them because they tell me the buyer is interested at some level. See if you can put together a deal that works for both of you. If you determine it doesn't make sense for you, that they won't come off their price, they are demanding too many changes or the changes are too costly, then you can walk away. But don't walk away without trying to make a deal work.

You also want to negotiate the terms, not just the price. In some cases, just like when we're negotiating to buy a piece of land, for builders the terms may also be more important than the price. For example, maybe you have two offers. One is $5,000 more than the other but it is contingent on the buyer selling their house, or getting financing, or a long option period. And the other one is an all-cash deal that can close quickly after a seven-day option period. The second one is much more likely to close, and quickly, while the first may never actually happen. In this case, unless I'm currently in a relaxed financial position, I'd accept the deal that is $5,000 less.

The process of negotiating and accepting an offer must not be too slow but not too fast—"just right." The same way that I recommend not being so quick to walk away from an offer, I also recommend that builders not accept an offer immediately, therefore showing excessive eagerness or desperation, even if that's not the case. When you do that, you suggest to the buyer that they may have offered too much, even if they didn't, and you create the effect of buyer's remorse opening your buyer to start overthinking the deal. They may question, "Maybe we went too fast." "Maybe we offered too much." "Maybe we should keep looking—I don't like that our offer was accepted so quickly." Unless it's a very hot market, take a moment to evaluate the offer and avoid sounding awfully eager to accept it. This is a crazy game but it is a big-ticket item that can make most people nervous stressing over making a mistake.

Continuing with the craziness, on the flip side, if you drag out negotiations for too long trying to squeeze every possible dollar from your buyer, they may get frustrated and also walk away. Use logic, fairness, and common sense; don't try to nickel-and-dime them too much, it's not worth it.

My recommendation is to negotiate reasonably. Give what you can, but maybe not in the first round. Ask your agent, "What kind of buyer are we dealing with? Are they a straight shooter or a negotiator?" Some buyers enjoy the game and want to go back and forth three times, while others are more focused on getting the deal done. It's helpful to learn a little bit about the person you're negotiating with, to be able to give them the process they are comfortable with.

A trick for making deals is to find out what is truly important to the buyer. Your agent should be able to investigate. Do they want a smaller down payment, more features, upgrades, or maybe more time to close because they have an apartment lease? Find out what the other elements and considerations are, to better meet the needs of a buyer you would otherwise lose. Without information, you may be focusing on negotiating the wrong points. Maybe you're focused on lowering the price, assuming that's what they want most, when really what they need is more time to close. Or maybe the price is fine, the house is perfect, but their cash is tight and they're worried about closing costs, which you could assist with. Every deal is different so customize your negotiation.

Don't negotiate based only on what's important to you, which is basically selling the house for the highest price at the fastest time. Instead, find out what would make the house a perfect home for them and therefore a good deal.

The whole point of this exercise is to ensure that you understand everything involved in properly pricing a house. Do your homework and really investigate what will give you the highest level of competitiveness.

CHAPTER 11

Marketing Basics

This book is clearly not focused on helping you become a master negotiator, nor is it intended to turn you into an expert real estate agent. What it *will* do is help develop your sales skills, because selling your home is what will ultimately allow you to finalize the entire building cycle. Unless you are already a realtor or broker hoping to get into the construction business, you will be delegating this activity to someone else. Of course, you will still be participating in and very involved in making important decisions once the marketing efforts begin and as the offers come in. You may not necessarily be the one meeting directly with prospects, but you need to learn the game, how this product's consumer thinks, and what they expect.

Regardless of how many home sellers are under the impression that marketing and promotion impacts how quickly a home is sold, that hasn't been my experience. From what I hear other seasoned builders say, it hasn't been theirs either. Sellers may be dazzled by the promises their real estate agent makes about the incredible marketing they intend to do—all the advertising their listing agent is offering to expose to their home, the glossy flyers they'll be printing to blanket the area, the mass emails sent to thousands, the superb social media strategies and techniques, the huge advertising spread in a local real estate magazine, roadside billboards, or the fabulous snacks that will be served at the open house.

While all of this is very nice and certainly helpful, I think it's of lesser importance in selling your home. I don't think that these types of marketing or sales activities significantly increase your odds of selling a home. It can't hurt, but in my opinion, I have not seen those promotional activities make that big of a difference. Honestly, these kinds of tactics probably do more to promote the agent than the house.

Finding and connecting with buyers

What I've seen make a difference is offering the right value proposition with the perfect execution of the fundamentals, by paying close attention to each and every prospect. A real estate agent who has truly taken the time to learn and understand all about the house you've just built and its advantages, who can properly articulate them, be attentive, focused, knows the market, and, most of all, who is incredibly responsive by answering their phone, text, or email promptly, is going to make a positive impression and make someone more likely to buy from them—which means your home has better odds of being sold.

A representative on your side must be someone who has the same sense of urgency to sell your property. These are the agents who are very communicative, who invest time learning the technical information, who have the home on every real estate website known to man, have confirmed with their own eyes that the house is spotless every single time before showing it, and have assisted you in staging.

By the right value proposition I mean having it priced according to its characteristics, so you don't miss out on offers. The fact is that as long as you are properly listed in the MLS and in all other major search engines and real estate sites, you don't need to find buyers. I assure you that they will absolutely find you. For nearly every home buyer, a house is a very important purchase. For many, it's the single largest investment they will ever make. And for that reason, most buyers spend a lot of time ensuring that they don't miss visiting a single home withing their parameters. They investigate available properties, tour them, check out neighborhoods, and look at comparable properties. What you need to worry about is making sure that your property comes up in their search and that when your turn is up for them to come and see it, it shows perfectly. This is your one and only opportunity to shine, so your home better be in impeccable condition. The home must always look and show immaculately, from your signage being perfectly straight and well located, the fresh landscape on display, accurate showing instructions, good working keys with smooth hardware where no struggle is necessary, incredibly clean, touched up and smelling nice, all lights turned on, with your furniture and decor where it needs to be.

Rather than gimmicks, stick with tried-and-true strategies for making a good impression. Let me use my analogy of a restaurant again here to illustrate. When you open a new restaurant, chances are good that everyone within a mile or so radius is going to give you a shot. They'll come in to taste your food, check out the ambiance, and gauge whether they'll want to come back. The first time they step foot in your restaurant is your shot to make a positive impression. If you mess up, they probably won't be back. You only get one opportunity!

With new restaurants as with new houses, be more concerned about how you're presenting your product than how you're promoting it. What is the first impression you're giving? Are you welcoming? Is the service good? Do you invite your customers back for another meal? The details of that dining experience are similar to the experience buyers may have interacting with you or your real estate agent in the house you're selling. That first experience will matter so much more than whether you spent money on advertising in some newsletter. Your buyers will find you if your house meets even a few of their criteria.

Worry more about what buyers are going to see when they step into your house, and what they'll hear about it during the sales presentation than whether it's on the front page of the local community newspaper. What is your sales strategy, what is your elevator pitch, your brand identity, your story? Those are much more important long-term to your success.

Ensuring your house is picture-perfect at all times is also essential. Before a showing, walk through it, touch it up, and clean it to give the best first impression to potential buyers. If you choose to list the home prior to staging a model, which I do all the time, make sure that your agent and listing comments mention the fact that you are not done. Ask buyers to please disregard the mess just as you would do if a friend showed up unannounced, catching you off guard. That goes a long way because you are asking not to be judged just yet, communicating to the buyer that you still have work to do and that you care about the appearance of your home.

To be successful at marketing your property, you first need to know your house. This sounds simple but it's not. The key is to create a story around your house and why you built it the way you did. Buyers love stories, especially ones they can later repeat to their friends and family to explain some of the features of their new home and share why they chose it. So, think through how to explain why this floor plan is ideal for this lot, why you oriented the house the way you did, why you included certain architectural details, why you chose the appliances you did, and so on.

If you give your buyers the story of how the house came to be what it is, it can cause them to fall in love with it, because passion is contagious. Walk them through the logic of why you made the decisions you made about the house, such as the window sizes and placement, the wall color, or the roof materials. Romanticize the choices because you worked hard to make it all happen. "I saw this shade of blue when I was traveling through Greece a couple of years ago in such and such place and wanted to incorporate it into the shower," you could explain. Or, "I was in the Czech Republic at a bar and ran across this countertop that just blew me away, and I knew I wanted to use it here." Or, "I stayed at a hotel in Paris that had a faucet just like this, so I tracked it down and used it here." Of course, let's assume and hope that these stories are true, because that is normally how my wife and I get inspired by some of our selections. But even if the route to making your choices was much simpler, it doesn't matter. The point is to always show your enthusiasm and to try communicating your vision.

Providing this story is a lot like how an artist explains a painting. When you look at a painting, you may pick up on the colors and the general composition, but if the artist comes over and explains what he or she was thinking, what they were going through while painting it, and why those decisions were made, then you can appreciate the piece even more. You enter the world of the creator and connect much more with it.

One of the best ways to make a terrific first impression is to stage your home to perfection. That's why we called this an essential expense during our projections section. If you are building a community, then furnish one as your model home. Many builders avoid the expense of staging and I believe that's a mistake. The reason is that most buyers do not understand spaces; they can't think and visualize how large an empty room is, meaning they can't intuitively picture where their furniture could go in the space. They can't appreciate so many of the design decisions you made when the house is completely empty, which is why you should always stage the homes you're selling. Ideally, if you're building a development, you want a model home.

Within that model, you can show the most common floorplan you designed, and you can have it staged with furniture that perfectly fits the space and the scale of the house. Buyers can walk through it and really feel the space of your floor plan. And since the model home isn't being lived in, it is much easier to keep it looking spotless. Staging a model can make the difference between a sale or no sale.

MARKETING BASICS

Statistically, buyers will always end up spending more time in a furnished model than in an empty house. When we walk through an empty house, we tend to do it quickly, in and out, and move on. But when it's furnished, we analyze the details, pay attention to the use of the space, and may even sit down to relax and enjoy the rooms as we imagine what it would be like to live there. The simple act of being in the house for longer will trigger the part of our brain that generates the feeling of comfort, luxury, and a sense of ownership. So, you need to furnish a house for it to sell better and faster, assuming it's done right, because buyers can't visualize what the home will look and feel like without typical furnishings in place. When appropriate, you need to put the king bed in the primary bedroom to confirm for buyers that size bed easily fits, for example, and you need to place a table that seats six in the dining room to confirm the room is more than large enough to fit their family. You have to present the home perfectly staged, the way you envisioned it, so that they can appreciate it. Otherwise, they'll struggle.

It's not about just filling the space, but staging it with furniture and décor pieces that accentuate the positive in each room. Sometimes that means measuring down to the millimeter the space between the chair and the door—can someone walk through there easily? Does the door open correctly? Is the credenza centered properly on

---

Do keep in mind that the staging company's job is to rent you furniture, not to sell your home. There's a potential conflict of interest there you should be aware of. They may place expensive furniture in your entry-level property that ends up making the space look ugly or clustered. Don't do that. Make sure the rented furniture is appropriate for the house, as well as for the scale and design of the rooms. They should enhance the space, not overpower it. Always approve what's in every room and don't be shy about requesting certain pieces be exchanged if they don't feel right. Don't just focus on looks but also on functionality.

---

the wall or is it too tall, and do we even need a credenza to begin with or is it just crowding up the place? Does the light fixture need to be centered with the room or with the table or relocated all together?

All of these decisions about how to make the house you've just finished building look its absolute best to the potential buyers who come through are, to me, much more important than spending money on advertising. Sure, the photo may look lovely, but that ad, with your agent's name on it, is going to do much more for them and their business than it will do for yours.

What you need is the right product, the right value proposition, and the right agent to sell your house. Every dollar you have needs to be put into your product, into the house. I'd rather give a buyer a refrigerator or money for blinds or other allowances because that money is better spent on selling the home than on advertising.

Essential marketing tools

The next most important marketing tactic you need is great photos of your listing. Also, you have to do open houses—they bring in a lot of traffic to see your home. That may include brokers' open houses, to show off your home to real estate agents in the area. They're the extension of your representatives, since they have potential buyers, so you want and need them to see your great home.

When you hold an open house, I recommend holding them as often as possible. Some agents only hold open houses on one weekend day, but I prefer both days. And only schedule them once the house is done and perfectly staged—not before.

Typically, the brokers' open house is held on a weekday before the first public open house. These types of open houses help you get feedback from agents on your price, what they see, what they like, and what they don't like. And if you're not getting feedback, make sure to ask for it. It's okay if what you hear isn't 100 percent positive—hearing what they didn't like can be just as helpful in making tweaks that will make the house easier to sell. For example, maybe the brokers didn't like the brass finishings and wished they were silver. That's an easy fix. Or maybe they would have preferred curtains were hung on the huge picture window out back. Again, an easy fix. Of course, you don't want to rush over to make changes just because someone didn't like something, but when you hear the same objection over and over, it might be time to pay attention.

But you will never know about these issues unless you ask. So, after your brokers' open house and after each client showing, make a point of asking agents what they and their clients thought. Being told the client is "still looking" is a non-answer; it tells you absolutely nothing. Ask what their impression of the house was. Is it too big, too small, too much money, too far from work—why didn't they buy it on the spot? That's essentially what you want to understand. How did it not meet the buyer's needs and can you do anything to address it?

It's also useful to stay on top of what's for sale in your neighborhood and what has recently sold. You can fairly easily get a report on the MLS, Zillow, or Trulia regarding what has recently gone pending. So, what I do, or what I ask my agent to do, is contact the agent that sold a house that you consider to be a direct competitor to yours and ask why their client chose that house. Everything that goes pending in my market, in my price point, in my style, in my area, I want to know about. First, did those buyers even consider your house? Why or why not? And what made the difference between buying your house and the one they ended up with? This information can be a gold mine and help you sell yours more quickly.

In many cases you'll learn that there was nothing you could have done. Maybe the other house was in a better location or had a bigger yard. You can't fix that. But other things you can. By asking about competing homes that sold you can begin to educate yourself, so that your home will be the next one to go to pending.

Cross-selling, or talking to other agents in your market, should become part of your standard procedure. Get to know them so that you can become allies. Now, when you have multiple houses for sale in an area, if a buyer doesn't like one home, you can say, "Let me show you my other house, just down the street." That way you don't waste the traffic you've attracted. But if you're just getting started, you can use the same opportunity to refer a buyer to an agent-friend of yours who has a property for sale nearby. Referring traffic to other agents is one way to become very well-liked and well-known.

Understanding buyers' expectations

Unless you're dealing with that rare custom home buyer with a very generous or even unlimited budget, money is always a concern when buying a house. Before you start selling buyers on your product—the house you've just built—it's important to keep in mind a few things about them. Number one, many buyers are nervous. This is a huge investment and they're anxious. Number two, many of them are indecisive, because they often haven't gone through this process, and they don't really know what they want or what to expect for their budget.

Most buyers start the homebuying process with unrealistic expectations. They start out wanting or expecting to find something that may not even exist for what they can afford. Let's say they want a four-bedroom, three-bathroom home with a big yard and a pool, in a certain school district, and their budget is $350,000. As they begin their search, they realize that a house with all those characteristics goes for no less than $390,000, at which point they will have to come to terms with reality. They'll either need to come up with more money or reduce their demands. It's often the agent's job to help educate each of their clients to better understand what they *can* expect to get for their money.

As a result, they can quickly get overwhelmed. Some will suffer from decision fatigue; there are just so many factors to consider and their needs and wants may shift the more homes they see.

Of course, the more inventory, the more options they have, the harder their decision becomes. In a seller's market, with few homes available to choose from, the more decisive buyers become, out of necessity. If they delay, they'll lose out. Eventually they learn to compromise and shorten their wish list to prioritize and identify what they truly need instead of what they want. They may start with a list of twelve requirements that will soon enough be reduced to four.

Thankfully, most people are reasonable and understand that they have to make trade-offs based on their budget.

The point I'm trying to make is that if your house happens to be shown during the early part of a buyer's tour of what is on the market, they may very well be unimpressed. But don't be surprised if once they complete the rounds and see everything available at what they can afford, they might come back and select yours.

As it's commonly known, today's buying experience begins online. As I mentioned earlier, professional photos of your house are essential for your success. Before buyers are willing to come take a look at your property in person, you need to entice them with gorgeous photos of the exterior and interior of the house. Buyers make a decision regarding their level of interest in a matter of seconds, and a bad or unappealing photo can turn them off almost instantly. Make sure the angles and perspectives are optimum, everything is clean, uncluttered, and the lighting is bright, so as to make your rooms shine.

The same is true of video. Today, buyers want a virtual tour of your home, to check out all of the rooms from the comfort of their home or office before they decide whether to tour it. Make sure photo and video evidence of your house makes people want to come take a look at it.

Buyer personalities

Yes, we all have a buying personality and yes, we're all different. Our priorities, concerns, reasons for buying real estate, and life situations all vary. A smart thing to do when selling a product of this magnitude is to tap into some information regarding your buyer's purchasing circumstances. Get to know what's going on with each of them individually so you can address their specific needs, customize your presentation, and help them make decisions.

I've been very fortunate to be able to run my business from a unique vantage point, which has helped me really understand buyer decision-making. Here's what I mean: the vast majority of builders are small entities that typically negotiate a handful of transactions each year, at best. Then on the other side of the spectrum you have your large companies, with management layers and sales departments that operate within predetermined parameters. If the deal fits within that box, the sale happens; if it doesn't, there's no sale. Then there's me, with a sizeable number of regular transactions, with no rules, just basic survival instincts.

My company was producing significant sales volume, yet still small enough where I personally went back and forth through many agents simultaneously, passing on messages of what to say, what to accept and what to decline, making decisions. I did that not because the agents weren't qualified, but because the houses were mine, in different neighborhoods, and at different price points.

As a seller, you know the ins and outs of the financial circumstances surrounding your decisions. After going through this exercise hundreds of times, with so much at stake, you begin to develop a sixth sense about purchasing patterns and trends. When you combine that with what you already know about the current market, that knowledge allows you to increase the odds of making a sale.

When you start negotiating, some of the basic pieces of information I would try to gather from the buyer or from their agent include:

+ What are their current housing circumstances? Are they renting? Are they currently floating around because they've already sold their last place?
+ Are they first-time home buyers?
+ Are they cash buyers? Do they have financing in place?

- How is their credit?
- Have they been prequalified and at what price point?
- What amenities are they looking for?
- How far away is their workplace, or do they work from home?
- What's important to them in a house?
- How does my house meet their needs?
- Does my price meet their criteria?
- Are they relocating from another city?
- What's their age group?
- Are they empty nesters or do they have children, and what ages?
- Do they have pets?
- What are their hobbies?

Collecting answers to these and many other questions will allow you to understand their family and housing situation up-front, which can help you gauge how serious they are or how to more effectively present your product.

Nervousness during the buying process can manifest in many ways. One way is by the buyer throwing you a lowball offer, another is by being overly demanding. They may play tricks, suggesting that they don't love the house and they're almost doing you a favor by buying it. Some will ask for unreasonable requests in order to get closer to their idea of a perfect house.

I won't pretend to be a psychologist or to have the slightest understanding of the human brain. I will not claim to be an expert in behavioral science either, but I've sold enough properties and negotiated a countless number of transactions to have been exposed to an abundance of deal-making styles, strategies, and techniques. I've seen it all.

As a result, I will say that it doesn't hurt to attempt to understand what's going on with your prospect. Fortunately, most buyers are pleasant to work with and excited about their purchase, and of course, so should you be. I have created a very limited sample list of some popular purchasing patterns that I have encountered:

- The artist, who loves the basic house but who is also very much into design, color, texture, space, and has a vision that will perhaps require additional customization to complete the picture they have in their mind for what it could be.
- The negotiator, who likes the process of going back and forth with proposed prices in search of the very best deal. They want to squeeze as hard as possible, because this is their process, and it is necessary for them to believe that they got the absolute best price.
- The technician, who is mainly focused on how the house was built, the general features, and who will make every attempt to find something that was overlooked or could have been done better.
- The poker player, who will throw numbers at you with little explanation behind them, who will wait patiently for your reaction, expecting to learn from each of your moves and brilliantly close you instead of the other way around.
- The busy person, who's often unavailable as part of negotiating, is always difficult to get ahold of, claiming to constantly be traveling or in meetings, constantly blowing you off. Is that true or not? Who knows? Are they serious or not? It's hard to tell, but if you apply patience and not show desperation to make a sale, you will eventually succeed.
- The methodical, who will overthink the process to death and also cannot be rushed in any way, shape, or form. This buyer is ready to pull the trigger but also willing to spend as much time and even lose a deal or two for the sake of reaching the much-needed comfort level to finally move forward.
- The looker, who is serious about buying a house, but would not openly admit it in order to remove some of the pressure applied by your persistence and desire to make a sale. They will communicate things such as, "I may be ready in six months to a year, but I want to see what's out there." You

could not believe how many homes I've sold over the years to people who were not quite ready yet.

I don't mean to generalize, because there's everything in between, as there are certainly an endless number of us with our very own unique identity, but these basic examples give you a picture of types of buyers you could encounter. It's very possible to address their concerns or participate in their negotiation when you learn to work well with people and to determine what some of your buyer's characteristics are.

Negotiating a sale

Because of everything we just covered, no negotiation should ever be treated the same because they are all different in their own way. Only after you understand a consumer can you accurately make your case. So, let's back up for a minute.

Once a buyer has decided that your house is the one for them, the offer comes in and the negotiations begin. Of course, you've been preparing for this day for months as you've endured a long and, at times, difficult road.

Due to all the blood, sweat, and tears you've put into the house, it's easy to get emotionally invested and attached to it, and I don't mean in a "I can't let go of my house" sad way but in a "I won't sell unless I get what I deserve" proud way. You need to remember that this is your company's product. It's not your pet or your great-grandmother's necklace you're negotiating. It's not a piece of art either, and you really shouldn't attach any additional amount to the price tag because of your hard work, risk, or simply because it's your creation. In home building you can't charge a premium for effort.

If you become stubborn, you run the risk of losing a sale. You need to keep in mind that the market sets the price of your house and not just you, the builder. No matter how much you may want it to sell for more, if the market indicates it is not worth more, rarely will someone pay what you say they should. *You don't set your price, the house prices itself.* The weird thing about this product is that it's not priced based on the amount of time you put into it, but on comparables, the end-result, and market conditions.

Another thing to be aware of is that a house is a perishable product. It has a shelf life just like those bananas you just bought. As I warned early on, the longer that house sits on the market, the staler it gets. It starts rotting. The landscaping starts dying, things start getting damaged and deteriorated, and it gets run down from all the traffic traipsing through it. And then people start wondering why it's been sitting there for so long. "What's wrong with it?" they start to ask.

One common failing of some builders is that they will only finish ninety-five or so percent of a house and get distracted by a new project that is starting. They move on when they haven't finished the final details. You can't have a house that is even slightly unfinished and expect to maximize its appeal. Buyers don't like how an unfinished house looks, for the most part, unless it's at a fixer-upper price point. So, until the house is 101 percent done, don't move on to your next deal and meanwhile, acknowledge that it's unfinished during your presentation.

Many builders get fatigued toward the end and move on before cleaning up and sprucing up the house. They figure that since they're going to have to come back through after it sells and take care of items on a punch list, which are minor corrections and repairs listed by the buyer, they'll do it then, not now. That's a mistake that could cost you a sale. The house won't present as well if it's not pristine and sparkling. There should be no repairs or clean-up to be done before an open house. Otherwise, the buyer may question craftmanship. They may try to use the lack of appeal as leverage in the negotiation, or simply dislike it, not even understanding why.

After all, when you walk into a new-car showroom, you're presented with bright, shiny, clean cars to consider, right? They're

MARKETING BASICS

not dusty and dirty and missing pieces or panels. They're ready to drive off the lot. The same needs to happen with houses. Don't show a muddy, unclean house and expect that it will yield the same impression.

Even before you receive a written offer, it's likely negotiations have already begun. Agents often ask questions on their clients' behalf about your flexibility on certain terms, such as pricing, move-in date, help with closing costs, or repainting certain rooms. Questions from agents indicate their client is at least interested, though it's always unclear until they submit a written, binding offer.

In rare instances when you get the sense that the buyer is going to be high maintenance, either now or in the future, you should take that into account. If you know that the buyer can potentially be a problem, you might even choose not to work with that person. Because they're already whining about everything, it might consume you and you're entitled to walk away. The reason why I point this out is because you're not selling a T-shirt or a scarf with little to no consequences. This is a complex product with liability behind it that can haunt you down the road.

You want to work with reasonable consumers. The last thing you want is someone who will relentlessly continue to bug you with unusual requests that are not part of the sale. If they're

---

Earnest money contracts are designed to protect the buyer more than the seller. There are several situations outlined in the contract where the buyer can terminate the deal, such as through title objections or an option period. Sure, they may lose their earnest money if they miss that deadline, but there are ways they can back out even at the last minute, as late as the actual day of the closing. The seller cannot. There are almost no conditions under which the seller can cancel a signed contract. There is a clause that allows buyers to sue if the seller refuses to go through as agreed upon. Once you sign a contract, you're stuck with it, so take your time to review it and be careful.

---

complaining now about every little imperfection and demanding discounts, it's likely that behavior will continue after the sale. It may not be worth your time to engage at all with this type of buyer if you are not desperate for a sale. One of my philosophies is to only sell homes to people who are very happy about the purchase. I don't want someone to buy and live in one of my houses if they are not excited about it.

Let me reiterate that I always treat every written offer I receive with respect. I'm flattered, and I let the potential buyer know it. Even the ridiculous ones that I've seen some builders laugh at—that's just not my style. I am not saying that I'll accept them, but I am humbled and excited by them, because they validate my work regardless of the dollar amount. I'm also appreciative and respectful because they took the time and effort to at least write it up and give it a shot. Any offer is a compliment and I genuinely feel gratitude with every deal, even if they end up not working out.

You may be surprised to hear how many times I've been able to turn a low offer into a solid one, but it all starts with respect and appreciation. Some buyers, as I said, start super low with the understanding that they will have to come up in price in order to get the property. They figure it can't hurt to start at the bottom. Realizing that, I'm willing to counter to see how far they'll come up. In many cases, they get vested into the process, creating this unspoken sense of ownership to the point where they eventually end up moving into acceptable territory. But that only happens because I wasn't arrogant or insulting, and I was willing to work with them.

I would never encourage agents to bring me lowball offers, but if a buyer insists on starting out that way, I don't discourage it either. I know many builders don't want to hear them. They may even tell agents, "If it's not above this price, don't even bring it to me." I think that's short-sighted. I want to see all the offers and understand why the buyers thought their number was fair. At least that way you start a conversation where you listen to their side of the story while having the opportunity to explain why you think your price is fair. You get access to the buyer, whereas if you refuse to even consider to be open minded, you might just miss out on a perfectly good opportunity to make money, not to mention making someone's homeownership dream come true. Yes, as foolish or idealistic as it sounds, at the end of the day, that's what it's all about.

Additionally, by considering all offers, you can even use those to prompt others to submit offers, creating competition. Although some buyers don't like bidding wars and hearing about other offers discourages them, when it happens, many of them don't want to miss a chance to buy the house.

You can call other agents who have shown the house to test how interested their buyers are. In these multiple offer situations, as diplomatically as possible, I simply tell the truth, something like, "I have X offers but we're not quite where we need to be, so there is still time for you to jump in."

More often than not, people want what they can't have and hearing about other offers validates their interest or their appreciation for the house, because other people also like it.

There have also been cases where I've accepted above-asking-price offers in a hot market, signed the deal, and only then did the buyer decide that, "Maybe we're not ready for this," and back out. The problem in those situations is that by then, I've lost the other buyers who had been interested. So, one thing I try hard to gauge with every buyer is how serious they are. Are they truly interested in buying my house and are they able to close? That is, do they have their financing in place and are they requesting a short option period, which reduces the chance that I'll miss out on other potential buyers during that window?

Choosing to accept the highest price offer isn't always the best decision, is what I'm trying to warn you. You want to weigh your need to sell now with potentially risky buyers who seem seriously interested but who may not be able to pay top dollar. Asking questions about what they most like about the house can help you get a sense of how invested they already are in living there. The higher the emotional attachment to the house, the greater the odds that they will close, as long as financing is already pre-approved. I personally opt for the right buyer as opposed to the highest number and in a multiple offer situation, I can achieve that by requesting strong terms that leave little to no chance for the chosen offer to walk away. For example, if they are willing to waive the option period, raise the earnest money, or shorten the inspections period, then that shows a great level of seriousness and commitment to the house.

Once again, I recommend being methodical in how you approach selling homes. An elaborate thought process can improve your strategy and give you an edge time after time.

CHAPTER 12

After the Sale

Let's begin with the term "making a sale" and explore what it means in this particular industry. This simple statement has a slightly different meaning in home building than in other situations.

When you walk into your neighborhood café, grocery store, service station, dry cleaners, or shopping mall, it is more self-explanatory. A sale is a simple transaction. You go over to the cashier, you pay, and leave.

In the case of buying a home, it's not quite that simple. There are multiple steps and a sequence of events—almost layers of comfort—that get us closer to that final sale. It is more like a romance that develops over time. That initial step of putting an offer on a property is a serious step but only the first token of interest, kind of like dating. But it doesn't mean marriage yet. A first date, although exciting and promising, is still a long way from a wedding. There are still a number of things to do before you officially walk down the aisle.

Once you finally have an acceptable offer in-hand, after going through proper negotiations and having been signed by both parties, it may feel like your job is done. You designed, permitted, built, and sold the property, after all. But you're not done yet.

Getting that signed contract is Step 1 in closing the deal. Granted, yes, it's a huge step forward, but it's not the end of the road. Offers that turn into contracts are the starting point of another process you need to navigate before closing.

Although you're not on the hook forever, you certainly are for at least some time after the closing. Remember that there are many players involved in assembling a house, but you are the face representing it and the most accountable for its proper functioning.

Going above and beyond

By now you may feel like you've bent over backwards making this sale a reality for your buyers, but it is critical that you continue to be accommodating and accessible to them. Going above and beyond will significantly improve the odds of this transaction going through, because you've reduced any reason for your buyers to want to back out. That's the biggest threat at this stage of the game.

After the contract is mutually accepted and delivered to the title company with the deposit, the buyer's option period starts. What that means for you is that the deal is on the right track but not yet complete. Your buyer still has the option to terminate the deal for a number of reasons during a set number of days you've agreed on. Which is why you want to hold your buyer's hand and stay in regular contact to answer any concerns that come up during that seven- or twelve- or twenty-one-day window; whichever option term you agreed to. They can very easily back out during that timeframe if they find something that's concerning to them.

During their option period, you and your buyer need to complete a number of tasks and coordinate several professionals to get them done. These tasks include:

- ✦ Delivering contract and opening title
- ✦ Obtaining final financing approval
- ✦ Ordering an appraisal

- Ordering a property survey
- Obtaining and reviewing the title commitment
- Ordering an inspection
- Scheduling a preliminary walk-through of the house with you, the seller
- Completing all repairs requested on inspection report
- Performing a final walk-through

Buyers are normally responsible for scheduling most of these appointments, but you and your team will need to cooperate by responding to any questions and providing access to these service providers. That includes everyone from the surveyor to the appraiser, decorators, and anyone else who needs to go through the house. It's important to make these final steps your top priority and react promptly, addressing any concerns. The sooner these appointments happen, the sooner you can close.

In addition to making sure that you are familiar with the sequence of events, there are several other ways to go above and beyond from your buyer's perspective:

Be available. Make your buyer feel like they are the only people you care about right now by being responsive whenever they need you. Make them feel important and special. Don't disappear or stop communicating, no matter how busy you are. These appointments are standing in the way of you cashing out. Be easy to deal with.

Do what you say you'll do. Another way to do more than buyers expect is simply to do what you promised you would in a timely manner. Whether you've sold a house that was 100 percent complete, ninety-five percent complete, or even fifty percent complete, live up to your word. If you promised to be done by February first, or that you'd replace the tile they didn't like on the kitchen backsplash, or that you'd upgrade the dishwasher—do that. And if something has changed that has made it impossible for you to execute, communicate that as soon as possible after you learn about the issue. For example, if your landscaping crew can't get there this week, resulting in a week's delay until the grass is planted, tell your buyers now, before they go over to the house and find out on their own that nothing has been done. If the city inspector missed your appointment for the final walk-through, tell your buyer immediately, explain what that does to your completion date, and confirm that the appointment has already been rescheduled. Anticipate what their questions will be about how the change affects them and their plans. Because just as you're running around trying to coordinate all of your contractors and appointments, they're doing the same on their end with movers, cleaners, and other delivery services, and very likely have a deadline to move out of their existing residence.

Communicate often. Even after the buyer has agreed to let the option period expire and you're closer to the finish line, they still want regular reassurance that you're doing what you said you would. They want to see progress and evidence that you're completing the pending tasks. Which means that if, for whatever reason, something falls behind schedule—like work crews on-site addressing items on the punch list, city or utility company issues, or repairs following the inspection—inform your buyers before they worry. Because when they hear nothing, they immediately assume that you are irresponsible or that something is wrong, and their anxiety increases unnecessarily.

The antidote is simple communication, as often as possible.

Inspection reports

First and foremost, you should know that the role of the inspector, in addition to "inspecting" the house, is to provide their opinion about certain things. Just like attorneys trying to interpret the law in a court case, this can feel a little bit like that at times. It's always possible for things to get sticky over an item, creating confusion for no reason, and it's your job to calm everybody down. In some cases, inspectors will point items out that are perfectly fine but may not be the inspector's preferred way to get something done. Inspectors are detailed and many will make comments, really, because that is their job. However, they don't always refer to the standard or the rule, but simply state their opinion. You may want to offer an explanation of why you did some things a certain way to alleviate their concern.

When the inspector writes up their report, you can simply verify which items are code violations and must be corrected, and which are merely observations and opinions. You'll want to address everything the inspector has pointed out, either to clarify for your buyer whether the way the work has been done is safe and acceptable and why, or to confirm that you will take care of whatever imperfection has been found. Don't let the inspector derail the sale.

When you have the report in-hand and know what items must be corrected or changed, let your buyer know your schedule for the repairs. Many buyers don't want to let the option period expire until you respond to the inspection report, to confirm you will make the repairs. Some may take it a step further and ask you to make the repairs prior to the expiration of the option period, but in most cases, as long as there is a written agreement on what will or will not be done, everyone can move on. You may even run into a buyer who squeezes some last-minute "after-the-fact" renegotiations to compensate for any deficiencies found on the report that, even if irrelevant, could be used as leverage for them to request something else. They might agree to ignore the opinion of the inspector in exchange for that small upgrade they were thinking of, a nicer light fixture in their dining room, high-end sconces in the master bathroom, or a refrigerator.

Understanding your ethical and legal responsibilities

As with everything else in life, there's a fine line between legal and ethical responsibilities. Home building is no different. Over the course of building, selling, and beyond, every so often you will be faced with the dilemma of identifying whose fault it is when something goes wrong.

Problems have a way of showing up even when you aren't looking for them and you need to deal with them quickly. Ignoring them will only make matters worse. Regardless of whether it was your crew, a contractor, the weather, a government agency, a sudden change in regulations, the inspector, or just a situation outside of anyone's control, you are inevitably caught in the middle and being blamed. To what extent is it your duty to come to the rescue? What's fair and where do you draw the line? Having your moral compass pointing in the right direction can go very far in minimizing consequences.

Although everyone else may point fingers, elude, and avoid any kind of responsibility, don't automatically do that. You will learn to quickly determine when something falls within your jurisdiction and when you can comfortably forward the responsibility to the right party. Your ability to evaluate the scope of a problem may allow you to handle things even if they aren't your fault, because a dispute over something minor may not be worth it.

You certainly don't want to be taken advantage of by vendors, contractors, or buyers, but when you are moving along with a project or close to a sale, it often makes sense to solve problems and wrap up your transaction rather than try to place blame. It's better and less costly to make an effort to save an existing contract than to have to start all over again. Starting from the beginning means relisting the house, showing it, finding a buyer, and then going through the closing process. As long as it's within reason, I generally try to make my current buyer happy.

After the closing, when the house has officially sold, it's still a good idea to try to keep the new owner happy. That's how you earn a reputation for going above and beyond. Having buyers rave about the amount of care and attention you paid to them is valuable for your business. It helps build valuable credibility and customer satisfaction.

This means that if a buyer emails a month after the sale has closed to ask for help with something minor, you may want to cooperate. Our standard procedure was to send a maintenance person out to a newly built home within a few months after closing to do any minor fixes, like nail pops or paint touch-ups. We did this as a courtesy to our buyers, to make their life easier and to ensure they continue to be happy with their purchase. We also try not to do it more than once, but greasing a squeaky door or tightening a door handle is such an easy task that we would almost always say "yes" when a buyer requests help.

We did ask that they first put together a list of things they want adjusted, so that our team could take care of it in one trip, rather than having to come back four or five different times.

If any of the repair requests are the domain of one of your contractors, such as an issue with the air conditioning or with the floors, you should contact the contractor who did the work and ask them to go back and correct the problem. The reputable ones will have no issue going back to the house, but it can take some prodding once in a while. Like you, your contractors thought their work was done; they've been paid and moved on to other projects. Having to now stop work on a new project to go back and deal with a customer that is not paying them any extra money is not their favorite thing to do.

Of course, if you have an ongoing relationship with the contractor and they know you have other upcoming developments for them, they may be very willing to do what is necessary to keep you and the buyer happy. But you have less leverage if this is the only time you used that contractor and they know they are unlikely to get future work from you no matter what they do in this specific instance. Getting them to act may require some persistence on your part.

Avoiding lawsuits

You certainly didn't choose home building to spend time dealing with problems, but when you're in business it's inevitable. Ultimately, you need to pick your battles and most importantly learn how to prevent them. Sometimes it's worth doing a little extra even if it's not your responsibility simply to avoid having the situation escalate to a dispute. You don't want that, mainly because it will take more time and money. You want to build goodwill throughout the sales process in order to avoid having to have a judge decide who is right and who is wrong. For example, if a tile has broken in the first few weeks of occupancy or the floor got scratched and it's easy to fix, just fix it. A quick trip over to take care of small problems like this will serve you well in the long run. An hour spent taking care of small things can help you avoid having to spend many more hours on legal negotiations or bad reviews over problems for which your buyer blames you.

Disputes rarely reach the courtroom and most often settle prior to or during a mediation, but you still want to avoid the expensive process. A tip I offer for avoiding problems in court is documenting everything you do. And I do mean everything. Because if something ever goes wrong dealing with a buyer who cannot be satisfied, you have to be able to prove that you did your part.

That means that all negotiations, scheduling, visits, repairs, warranties, and changes need to be written down or typed up and signed, to indicate everyone's acknowledgement of what is being agreed to. So, if a buyer indicates they must have the front door color changed before move-in and you've agreed, it's critical that you type up that agreement, indicating what is being done, and then have the buyer sign it to confirm that is what they requested.

Only by collecting signatures from your buyer will you have proof that you did everything agreed upon. So that if you do end up in a dispute, you will have signed paperwork to back up your claims.

The process may sound super formal and contentious, but it's not. For example, if your buyer asks you to send someone to work on a malfunctioning light switch, you confirm via email that someone from your company will be at their house on Tuesday at 10:00 a.m. to repair the item. You need someone there to open the door. Then, when you get there, you take care of the problem and ask the buyer to sign a sheet of paper you've brought with you that documents what you did and when. You can say that the company requires it, to prove you went out on a service call.

This step may sound petty or unnecessary but it's not. Getting signatures indicating agreement that you were there and that work was attempted can be key in some states to your winning or dismissing a lawsuit. At a minimum, signed documentation shows that you made an effort. The buyer can't claim that they're being ignored if you can produce signed papers proving you came by four times to adjust something or to repair something. Courts want to see that you're being responsive, that you're attempting to correct the problem and do the right thing.

Above all, don't ignore problems or complaints from buyers, even if it's after closing. Those problems can only escalate and make your life more difficult. If someone calls you with an issue, make an appointment to investigate it, determine if the problem is covered by a warranty, and address it. All the while you should also be documenting what you did, when you went to check out the problem, what you did to investigate any applicable warranty, etc. These types of notes will be essential if you do end up going to court down the road.

Service quality and warranties

As a builder, you will offer your own warranty on the house you just built. That document, which you give your buyer, details what your company offers and what you are responsible for. That's what a warranty represents, after all—what you are responsible to repair or replace if it does not perform as expected during a set time period. That is, what parts of the house are warrantable, what conditions need to exist for a repair or replacement to be made, and how long the warranty is in force. Perhaps even more important is that within that document you need to describe what is *not warrantable*, or what is not covered by the warranty. It needs to be clearly stated what is covered and what is not.

It's also important to understand that if you pay an outside service to warranty the house you just built, you, as the builder, may still be legally responsible for various aspects of the house, depending on the state in which you reside, the warranty you offered, and the item in question.

Many builders buy additional warranties for their buyers to protect everyone. This is more common in the resale market, when the buyer is purchasing an existing home and wants to be sure that things will work after closing. But these third-party warranties are all different and you must understand what you're buying.

Because some warranties only cost a few hundred dollars, they are very appealing. However, they are not really full warranties. Most of these services are more like third-party inspections. For a few hundred dollars they will send an inspector out to evaluate if the problem is warrantable or not. But that product does not actually cover the cost to make the repair if it is deemed to be covered by a warranty. An actual third-party warranty is typically a few thousand dollars and does include the repair or replacement of defective elements of the house. The cost is generally calculated based on the price of the house and the square footage, times a percentage.

Know what you're buying and how it works before you pay for something that will not offer the coverage you're expecting.

Some of the struggles that arise are when problems are discovered long after they originated. Such as when something that was warrantable in year one is discovered four or five years later. Some buyers will try to get coverage for the repair or replacement that they should have reported in the first 365 days but didn't, and you may need to argue it. The good news is that chances are that you are not liable because buyers had the opportunity to properly inspect the house and once the year runs out, it is likely that you are no longer responsible.

Many first-time home buyers have no sense of what kind of regular maintenance should be done on their house. They've never owned property before, so they simply don't know, and even if they do, it never hurts to remind them. A simple solution is for you to provide a list of maintenance recommendations prior to closing. These are easy tasks to address regularly that will also prevent large problems down the line; otherwise, buyers may end up completely ignoring important preventive measures. This is very similar to scheduled services done to a car or a boat, which are exposed to the outside environment.

Neglecting to provide this information may backfire by the buyers assuming that there are flaws with the house or that the builder is supposed to come back and take care of all this as part of the warranty. Meet with your construction team and create a full itemized recommended maintenance schedule for your buyers according to the style, design, and specifications of the home. This will clearly establish what is their responsibility, prevent confusion, and preserve their home.

Differentiating warrantable items from non-warrantable ones can be tricky. Convincing a buyer that an item represents wear and tear, caused by hail, windstorm, hurricane, or lack of maintenance, as opposed to a warrantable issue or defect can be challenging. It is important for you to make these as clear as possible up-front. The builder is obviously the path of least resistance when something goes wrong because calling the insurance company can cause a deductible and possible rate increases. It is your job to investigate the incident and confirm if the damage was caused by actual defects or outside factors.

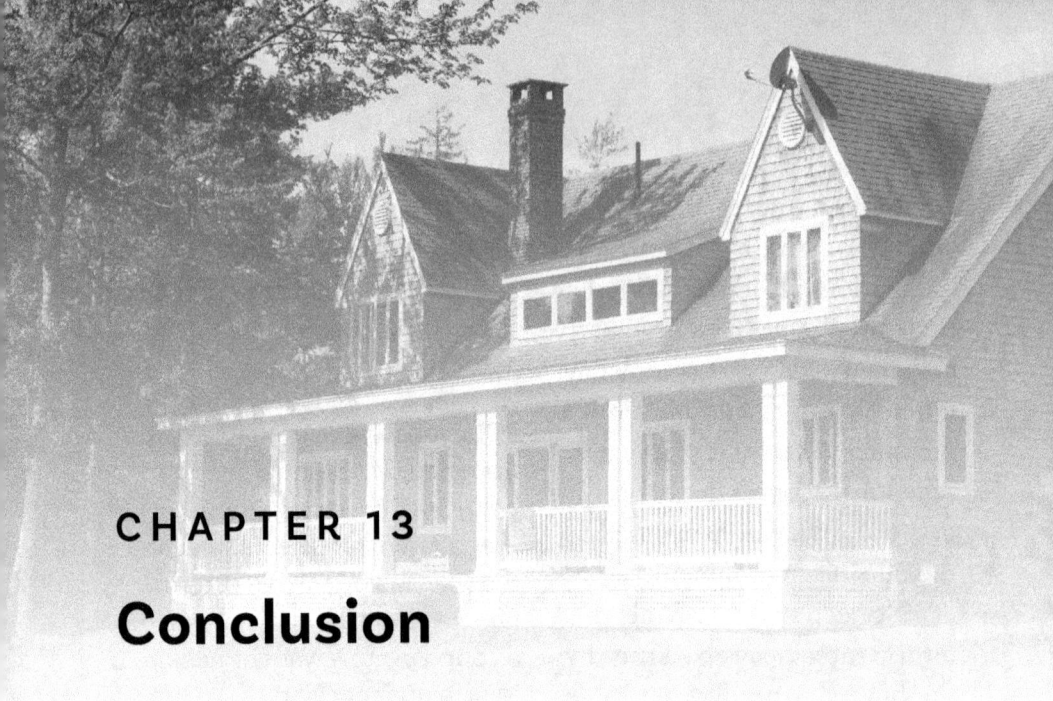

CHAPTER 13

Conclusion

One of my objectives for writing this book was not just to dispense advice regarding this particular field, but to share my love of entrepreneurship. This collection of thoughts and experiences is meant to go far beyond the scope of home building. It's written with the hope that you as the reader can use the information and translate it to any other product or service. With the right logic, all fundamental aspects of operating a business have similarities and much of this can be applied no matter where your journey takes you.

Now, as far as *The Business of Home Building* recommendations, it's very clear to me that one book is not nearly enough to discuss even a small fraction of what I've lived through in this industry. It would be impractical to attempt to include enough details regarding the full scope of what this business means—there's just too much to cover. But I do believe that this general guide will be eye-opening and provide you with some insights to be mindful of.

This book is my synopsis. Whether you recently got involved, are considering getting started in, or simply have an interest in the science of the home building business, I urge you to pay attention to the word "business" in that phrase. Remarkably, in the heat of the moment, that word gets overlooked and my message is that you cannot afford to skip steps and expect to stay in this industry long-term.

The excitement and anticipation of building and creating something that fuels your creativity might distract you from other extremely basic needs required to operate a company. When you become interested in some technical or artistic field, never forget to also focus on that other side of the equation—the business. Neglecting to do so can be catastrophic.

Now, let's assume that you're taking your first steps toward starting your home building business. I want to quickly review some of my top recommendations. If you've paid attention to the tone of this book, you may have captured a little bit of my love-hate relationship with this business, which is why I believe I am probably the perfect candidate to tell you all about it. I am not sugar-coating anything or trying to steer you in any direction. I am not trying to discourage you from exploring this fascinating world, but also not telling you that it's all fun and games. I obviously must like something about it to have stayed in it for almost three decades.

My goal here is to point out the good, the bad, and the ugly so that you can better make an educated decision regarding your future in home building. I want to help you get started on the path to profitability with the fewest number of challenges and surprises possible. Or at least allow you to think about things that may not have occurred to you while entertaining the idea of building homes.

One of the main messages here is that you must dive into every single aspect of this process before you get started. Consider learning at least the basics of all the areas, especially the ones unfamiliar to you. Otherwise, you will find out the hard way that it was a bad idea to avoid the subject and assume that building a good quality home was enough to succeed.

Devoting the appropriate amount of time to creating a business plan and outlining your objectives will serve as your most important tool of all. The simple action of sitting back, meditating, and organizing your thoughts about how you intend to execute your strategy is enough to get ahead of the game. Clarifying the reasoning behind why, exactly, it is that you are getting in this business will help you trace a better path to a bright future. Understanding your place within this competitive industry is crucial to making progress. This is not a sports team where the coach will identify your talent and then tell you what position you should play, or even if you should be playing the game at all. This is something that you will have to determine all on your own.

From carefully selecting a strategic business model that suits your needs to raising the right amount of capital, picking the correct product to build, hiring the best possible team, and learning how to manage them, as well as managing your own time, may be the difference between winning or losing.

There are many reasons why businesses fail, but one very common one is money, or, better yet, the lack of it. Either by neglecting to raise the appropriate amount of cash or by mismanaging it, money determines business success. When you think about it, there are truly few issues in the business world that cannot be fixed with money. Simultaneously, there are very few that can be fixed without it. Most problems stem from not having resources, which is why I place an emphasis on raising and managing your funds.

The art of estimating budgets, anticipating needs, forecasting possible obstructions, planning for setbacks, and knowing from what direction they can come at you is my message. One of the first pieces of advice I offer is that your personal need for money should not dictate your decision to enter this market. Don't just do it for money, there must be something deeper that drives you to stay in it for the long haul.

Before you get too far down the line, you also want to get clear about how you want to run your business. That often depends on the aspects of the industry you enjoy. For example, if you like designing and architecture, you'll play a different role than if you love financials. You need to ask yourself how busy you want to be. Do you want to build one house at a time or are you hoping to ramp up your operations quickly? That will certainly impact how you set up your operations from the outset.

And if your objective is quickly scaling your business, be ready for things to get worse before they get better. Many businesses also fail during their first attempts to grow because growth is a major source of instability and confusion. Expansion is a moving target that requires you to have mastered the balancing act.

You need to test your skills gradually to understand how you react to the multiple components brought on by growth and stress. Scaling is also a game of balance, where your infrastructure must evolve in sync with the amount of product that you wish to deliver. The equilibrium of investing in your projects is correlated to the investment made within the company's systems and operation. One cannot grow without the other or the house of cards falls apart.

Aggressive but realistic projections are necessary to push you and your team forward. Setting goals in every area of the organization is a daily task, from meeting deadlines, getting ahead of schedule, improving budgets, selling properties faster than expected, achieving progress, and obtaining permits the way you planned is your objective.

Be aware that choosing to pursue business growth requires that you invest more of your resources—your time, your money, and your expertise. To grow, you'll need to hire more contractors or laborers, buy more computers, move into larger office space, find more land to build on, and get more money for the projects you're selling. Eventually these investments will pay off, but not immediately. You need to have the financial stamina to continue paying your business expenses even when you may not yet have cash coming in, not to mention the ability to multiply yourself and become the most efficient person in the organization.

As the owner, you can't afford the luxury of investing too much time in one sector of the company. You must operate like a drone and always know what's happening in every corner of the business at all times. The personal and financial investment in your business must always come first, which can be painful if you don't have many resources to allocate. Fortunately, there is a solution if you have limited resources: slow your growth to a level that you are able to monitor.

We've discussed how instead of hiring employees who are paid regardless of their work flow, it is safer to outsource for most positions, at least in the early stages, because independent contractors are paid based on the job. You can tie their work to incoming cash to better manage your overall cash flow needs.

If you've opted to go the custom home builder route as your business model, you'll want to focus on perfecting your craft as opposed to volume. Scaling is limited in this scenario, because every single job requires an entirely new "everything," from style, quality, designs, selections, locations, and providing your clientele with the time and attention to deliver the home they're looking for. Where other types of builders scale up, custom home builders build a following or an audience. Your followers are your potential future buyers and you want to do all you can to slowly keep increasing the size of that audience, in order to make selling future homes possible.

While growing, I strongly urge you to picture where you want to be and work backwards to figure out how to get there. Building a business that constructs four homes a year is very different from one that produces 200 or more, and you need to start planning now if that's where you want to be. Also understand that your percentage growth rate is more important than the pure numbers. What I mean is, the process to grow from ten to twenty homes a year is very similar to growing from 100 to 200—in both cases you are doubling your production, or growing by 100 percent. This is particularly the case if you build in locations that are spread out geographically.

Trying to visualize the future, from your finances, bookkeeping, design, purchasing, construction, warranty, all the way to what that workspace or headquarters might look like is an amazing exercise, not to mention a powerful visualization technique. That's the best way to create a plan to reach your goals—by picturing it and then working backwards to figure out how to get there.

I remember when we were building twenty-five or thirty homes a year and working toward building 100. And once I could picture exactly what that size of company would look like, I could plan what staff I would need, what financial resources I would need, and what size office space we would need. It became an algebra equation, really. Once we hit fifty houses, I realized how easy it would be to ramp up the operation to get to 100. And we did.

Home building is a fascinating industry; scary but exciting. There is always something new to learn. It's never boring, that's for sure.

However, it is complex. As an entrepreneur, you need to be both a generalist, knowing a little bit about everything, as well as a specialist, becoming an expert in some aspect of your business. Otherwise, you will never progress beyond mediocrity.

What I mean is that you won't succeed by being good at only one thing. You have to be good, to some degree, at all of the aspects of your business. You don't have to be an expert at everything, but you need to understand the basics at least, to be able to judge the work that other people are doing. There may be some businesses where you can afford to only be good at one or two things, but home building isn't one of them. If you're an expert in one aspect of the business, all of the rest will perform poorly and you won't succeed.

You must remain open-minded, creative, and interested in staying up on the latest trends in home building. That way you can serve your clients, serve your contractors, and serve your employees. You need some technical understanding, business savvy, and a vision of what you want your business to grow into. You need to know how to market and sell, as well as to communicate orally and in writing. Passion and focus are required to maintain the energy and enthusiasm for the business long enough for your company to become profitable. You as the owner are the morale booster that fuels your team. You must have the determination and grit to keep going and not throw in the towel, and I can assure you that there will be moments when you'll want to. Every business can be excruciating at times, and the solution is to find purpose and a strong reason to stay. For example, my brother and I had each other, and as many moments got tough, I wouldn't walk away, I wouldn't let him down, and he did the same for me. This forced us to put up with more pain than most people can tolerate. And just like that, one fine day we succeeded!

Know that you're not going to make it big overnight, allow the process to take its course and learn from your mistakes.

You don't have to love everything about home building—I certainly don't! You can love some aspects and find reliable help for the others.

Remain frugal for as long as you can. Be stingy with your money *and* with your time. Don't buy things you don't need, don't pay for services that aren't essential to building your business, and don't waste time on activities that aren't revenue-generating.

I strongly urge you to watch your cash and not just today, but what you expect it to look like next month and next quarter. Keep an eye on your cash flow and forecast.

Watch your cash even more than your profits. You need cash to survive but you don't need the profits immediately. Profit can come later.

Your attitude in business affects more than you might expect. Positivity and optimism are key, mixed in with a touch of reality. Said another way, hope for the best but prepare for the worst. Nobody knows how the housing market will behave tomorrow, even less next year or the following. I don't care what the experts say, the only thing that is certain in this and in all other businesses is that things will constantly change and evolve. So, be skeptical when selecting your next deal, when you research a property, and when you make critical decisions. Take risks but take calculated risks. Make educated choices; don't be foolish by getting emotional.

And once again, document everything you do as you go and as much as you can. Don't operate with blinders that prevent you from looking at the broad spectrum of running a well-oiled organization. You are now playing in the big leagues, standing exactly where the great leaders of the world first started, and where everybody wants to be. You hold that special place in society that represents the American Dream, the ultimate symbol of freedom and victory. Don't let anything escape your attention, don't waste this incredible opportunity. You're no longer wearing one hat, with one job description, but instead you're on a mission, a dangerous expedition that demands powerful survival skills, surrounded with countless responsibilities where they all rely solely on your skills. You're now the boss, so act like it! Always have your eyes and ears *everywhere*. As they say in boxing and other combat battles, "Protect yourself at all times." If you're not ready to put your personal life on hold and give everything you've got to owning a business, I suggest that you don't waste your time. Yes, it will be difficult, borderline torturous at times but one day, when you look back at your accomplishments, you will be proud, it will all start making sense, and it will all have been worth it.

Do you recall back in those uncomfortable periods of time during final exams in school, when for a few days you had to pull yourself together, eliminate most distractions, put friends aside, leave bad habits alone, and replace all of those with pure clarity and focus to be able to clear up space in your brain to absorb all sorts of information? It was time to process solutions, memorize tons of things, find answers to overwhelming and sometimes impossible equations, learn difficult lessons, and swallow large doses of pressure. Well, owning a start-up business is a lot like that, other than it goes on for much, much longer, and there's also a lot more at stake. If you want the slightest chance of reaching the finish line, hopefully you'll understand that many sacrifices will have to be made in order to succeed. The good news is that at some point, you gets used to it and become a better entrepreneur, or at least that's the plan, because the alternative is to walk away and accept defeat, reducing yourself to live with regret. I certainly wasn't going to do that!

If you've ever played competitive sports, taught yourself a language, put together a symphony or a prize-winning Broadway production, or attempted to become a champion at something, you'll understand what I'm talking about. The truth is that at the end of the day, this is what life is all about—pushing yourself beyond your limits in pursuit of a higher standard of living. But if you're able to convince your mind and spirit that what you want is indeed possible, when you arrive at that place, life will become a more beautiful and fulfilling experience, because you'll know that you lived with passion and conviction.

That road you followed, which often felt dark and lonely, one day will become brighter and suddenly you're ahead of the rest who weren't able to sustain that horrible pace. You have empowered yourself to change the world, and to achieve things that most people could only dream of. You've become a figure, an authority, who commands respect and admiration, and who can now live life as you please. Only then will you have earned the right to switch gears and take on a new challenge of showing the next person the path to achieving their own dreams.

www.ingramcontent.com/pod-product-compliance
Lightning Source LLC
LaVergne TN
LVHW010201070526
838199LV00062B/4442